Strategic Planning Demystified

Performance and Customer Based Planning Approach

A planning method for any organization.

By Milton Laughland

© 2014 Milton Laughland   All rights reserved.

Manufactured in the United States. No part of this book may be reproduced in any form or by any electronic or mechanical means including information storage and retrieval systems without permission in writing from the Author.

First Edition
ISBN-13: 978-1-5024-0311-7

Cover designed by Royce Stewart

Special Acknowledgement:
Nell-Marie Colman - Editing
Mary Laughland - Editing
Bill Hopkins - Reviewer

Author may be contacted at miltlaughland@gmail.com

Disclaimer
This book is only a guide and not a substitute for tailored advice. Although an effort has been made to ensure the accuracy and completeness of the information contained herein, the author cannot and does not guarantee positive results. The author accepts no legal liability whatsoever arising from or connected to the accuracy, reliability, currency, or completeness of the material contained in this book or any sources to which the materials refer. The author assumes no responsibility for errors, inaccuracies, omissions, or any other inconsistency herein. The reader is responsible for his or her choices, actions, and/or results in using the suggestions contained herein. In reading this book, the reader agrees to be bound by this disclaimer.

Contents

Preface v

What Makes Strategic Planning Demystified Unique vi

Conventions vii

Major Definitions x

Overview xii

PART ONE: Why Strategic Plans Fail 1

    A.   Indicators of Failed Planning 1

    B.   Committees 5

    C.   Planning Is Not Cyclical 6

    D.   Arbitrary Time Periods 7

    E.   Timeline Mistakes 10

    F.   Vision versus Mission 13

    G.   Core Values 17

    H.   Poor Executive Management 19

PART TWO: Strategic Planning Demystified 23

    Four Key Elements to Planning 26

PART THREE: Strategic Planning 29

    A.   Executive Commitment 30

    B.   Mission Statement 31

    C.   Goal 48

    D. Objective 61

    E. Strategy 71

    F. PRMs (Performance and Results Measurements) 84

    G. Accountability to the Plan 101

    H. Organizational Alignment 105

PART FOUR: Strategic Planning Coordinator (SPC) 109

PART FIVE: Understanding Risk and Failure 113

PART SIX: Tactical Plan 121

PART SEVEN: Analysis 127

    A. Elements to an Analysis 131

    B. The Analyst 135

    C. Analysis Tools 135

PART EIGHT: How Strategic Planning Demystified Works 139

PART NINE: Visual Concept 147

PART TEN: Organization Size 151

PART ELEVEN: A Few Last Words 153

APPENDIX A: Mission Statement Examples 155

APPENDIX B: Vision Versus Mission 185

APPENDIX C: Government Performance and Results Act (GPRA) .. 195

APPENDIX D: Various Other Plans and Analyses 203

Preface

I worked for the Federal Bureau of Investigation (FBI) for over 32 years in various research, analytical, and management positions. The last 16 years were devoted to Strategic and Tactical Planning for the FBI's Criminal Justice Information Services Division's successful development and delivery of a billion-dollars worth of technology projects - automating the fingerprint process, upgrading the National Crime Information Center, and creating a criminal background check system for gun purchases. I analyzed work processes, organizational effectiveness, Performance Measurements, contractor performance, business practices, and future project and business opportunities. I helped initiate activity-based costing, user fee cost analysis, and earned value contract assessment.

Over time, I identified the characteristics that led to successful planning, and those that did not. I studied available Government Accountability Office and Office of Management and Budget documents that evaluated the effectiveness of other agencies' efforts to initiate Strategic Planning. I attended conferences with other Federal agencies to learn from their experiences. Working one-on-one with executive and mid-level managers, I identified planning approaches that focused on performance rather than on functions. In time, I became the subject matter expert on planning. I understand why Strategic Planning can be difficult to implement effectively and what elements are needed for successful planning.

After retiring from the FBI, I joined SCORE (Service Corps of Retired Executives), a non-profit association dedicated to educating entrepreneurs and helping small businesses start, grow, and succeed nationwide. SCORE is a resource partner with the U.S. Small Business Administration and has been mentoring small business owners for more than forty years. As a mentor, I have counseled numerous entrepreneurs, and observed that an organization's planning effort presents the greatest indicator of success or failure.

This book represents the lessons learned as a former FBI Strategic Planning Coordinator and a SCORE business mentor. By keeping the planning approach simple, clearly defined, and focused on results, organizations can successfully plan for the future.

What makes Strategic Planning Demystified unique

I wrote this book to provide an easily understood approach to implementing a successful Strategic Planning process and to avoid the mistakes that hinder successful planning. This book will give you:

- The key indicators for a poor or failing Strategic Plan.
- The four major elements required for successful planning.
- How to create an effective Mission Statement and the Goals, Objectives, and Strategies that support the Mission.
- Learn the importance and value of good Performance Measurements that disclose your organization's success.
- Key elements not usually included in other Strategic Planning methods.
- The various analysis tools that reduce uncertainty and provide the information needed for making good decisions.
- Numerous samples for Mission, Goal, Objective, and Strategy statements.
- A book that speaks in plain English when explaining Strategic Planning.

When I began Strategic Planning, I read books and took classes on the traditional Strategic Planning approaches. Over time, I observed that certain standard methods resulted in less than successful planning. Some approaches allowed people to avoid conducting the difficult analysis that needed to be done. Other planning activities became constrained or skewed by artificial borders and barriers placed upon them. In many cases, managers believed Strategic Planning to be a wasted effort and would not invest the time and resources needed to build and manage a good plan. Their planning document would ultimately be shelved or ignored. I also found that Strategic Planning would fail because of poor Mission Statements, weak Goals/Objectives, poor Performance Measures, too much focus on Functions, and/or poor leadership. Over time, I experimented to find new and successful planning approaches. I tested different methods at various management levels. Working one-on-one with staff and management, I identified the most important and successful elements to planning.

Once you have read and absorbed this book's approach to planning, you can't help but be better at Strategic Planning. Part One focuses on the predictors to a poor performing Strategic Plan. Knowing why plans fail will help you avoid these predictors. The rest of the Parts provide clear definitions, explanations, and step-by-step instructions. Knowing what works will help you produce a successful and meaningful Strategic Planning process.

Conventions

To produce an easily read and understood book, I've incorporated several generalizations to reduce wordiness.

- **Using the word "organization."** The word "organization" is used in a broad context to include for-profit business, non-profit organization, or government agency. Strategic Planning Demystified approach can be used by any organization.

- **Using the word "product."** Usually the word "product" implies a tangible item (e.g., toaster) and the word "service" implies an intangible item (e.g., legal service). The word "product" will be used generically to include "service." In some cases, the word "service" may be used if more descriptive.

- **Business and Non-profit Organizations.** In the business and non-profit examples, a generic descriptive name (e.g., computer company, retail store) was used for discussing Strategic Planning, not for discussing a specific company or its products/services. Some examples have been modified to emphasize a point of view. Readers should not quote, use, or represent these organizational statements as fact nor attribute to a specific organization.

- **Using key words.** The following keywords are used as proper nouns: Mission, Goals, Objectives, Performance Measures, Vision, Function, and Core Values. The accompanying words (e.g., Plan, Planning, or Statement) are also in initial capitals. When used as proper nouns, these words refer to their respective part of the planning process and not the generic use of the words.

- **Analysis.** After each Mission, Goal, Objective, and Strategy example, I've highlighted my own analysis or opinion under the title of "Analysis" regarding the example and stressing a particular point of view for instructional purposes.

- **Using the word "customer."** In writing this book, I needed one word to be all inclusive when referring to the person or group that will buy, use, receive, etc., an organization's end product. I decided on using the word "customer" to represent an organization's end user. Most organizations have speciality words that describe the ultimate receiver and destination of their product.

    - retail business: consumer
    - medical: patient

- professional services: client
- non-profit: community, recipient
- government: taxpayer, citizen
- sports: spectator, fan
- financial: investor
- technology: user

As you read the word "customer," mentally insert the name category for your end user.

- A hospital administrator would interpret the word customer as patient.
- A retailer would convert customer to consumer.
- A law firm would change customer to client.
- A college would replace customer with the word student.

Using the word "customer" as a generic term allows me to keep definitions and explanations short without having to attach a long list of end-user titles.

Another reason for using the word "customer" is the concept that all organizations have customers. Business organizations clearly understand the idea of a customer. The customer pays for and uses the product(s). Non-Profit and government agencies have difficulty accepting the concept that they have a customer. Non-Profit organizations tend to focus on issues and concepts (e.g., poverty, disease, social services). Government agencies believe they exist to conduct legislative-mandated Functions. Non-Profits and governments, in fact, do have customers. Customers define the product an organization needs to provide. Customers' success defines an organization's success. When an organization focuses on Function, the intended outcome on the customer may be lost or forgotten.

If government agencies look into the original legislation, they will find the name of the customer. Although the government appears to be trying to save the environment, the real customer is the American people. The ultimate Federal government Mission is to protect the American people against actual or perceived dangers to health, the economy, security, and other society issues. The U.S. Coast Guard realized years ago that its Mission was not to patrol territorial waters but was to protect and save lives. This shift in thinking made a significant improvement in the Coast Guard's approach to Strategic Planning.

Major Definitions

For the novice planner, the following Strategic Planning definitions provide immediate insight to the Strategic Planning Demystified approach. For seasoned planners, some definitions differ from what they have previously used. These concepts will be explained later in detail.

Definitions for the word Mission vary greatly. Most definitions for Mission use one or more of the "who, what, where, when, and how" approaches, leaving such confusion that no one has a clear definition of a Mission statement. I redefined the word Mission because it needed a clear and concise explanation. Vision is another word that I have redefined so that it is clearly distinguishable from Mission.

Mission Statement: A desirable and attainable end result for the customer.

Vision Statement: A desired but not yet attainable end result for the customer.

Goal: A major accomplishment or activity needed to reach or support the Mission.

Objective: A short-term, major activity for accomplishing a Goal.

Strategy: A concrete and specific action for accomplishing an Objective.

Performance and Results Measurements (PRMs): The results to be achieved for or by the customer.

Function Statement: The work or task conducted by an organization.

Core Values: How the organization treats its customers and itself.

Attainable: With sufficient resources and actions, a desirable end result can be attained by or for the customer with the organization's product.

Failure: Not attaining a desired or intended result or outcome, resulting in harm to the customer and/or organization.

Risk: An internal or external unplanned event that could negatively impact an organization's effort to achieve success.

Calculated Risk: A recognized risk in which an organization is willing to consider taking in an effort to achieve success.

Component: Division, Branch, Section, Unit, or other organizational structure found within an organization.

Stakeholder: A stakeholder is a person or organization (other than the customer) that has a stake in the organization's success.

Strategic Planning: Long-term planning in which resources may not yet be identified and/or committed.

Tactical Planning: Short-term planning in which activities and resources have been identified and committed.

< >

Overview

Planning is a human activity. We have short-term lists (e.g. grocery list) and long-term plans (e.g. save money for the kids' college fund). In some cases, we make short cryptic lists on paper or in electronic devices to keep us on schedule. We change our list or schedule when an event or new information requires us to change our plan.

For organizations, planning requires a formal, documented, and organized approach. Today's organizations continually face changes in supply and demand, the economy, stakeholder and customer requirements, technological advancements, government rules and regulations, production schedules, etc., which impact short- and long-term planning. Large organizations have multiple organizational layers (bureaus, branches, divisions, etc.) that must play nice with each other. For these reasons, many organizations create a Strategic Plan so they can work towards a common Mission using a set of Goals that will lead to success.

When an organization decides to create or update a Strategic Plan, something has happened to make management uneasy or unsure about the future. A sense of foreboding or fear that the organization is being overtaken by competition, technology, or some other real or perceived threat. The organization believes it needs to evaluate its status today and determine where it must go tomorrow to be successful. The organization brings its best people together to create a plan for future success. Good ideas surface, fresh new Goals appear, and a renewed energy arises. All this effort is documented on paper. But then something happens. Over time, the document becomes obsolete and stagnant and the Goals fail to be achieved or are simply forgotten.

Albert Einstein is alleged to have said that the definition of insanity is doing the same thing over and over again and expecting different results. If your organization had a Strategic Plan and is starting a new one, the organization should ask these questions about the old plan:

- Did the plan help accomplish anything?
- Did the plan drive the organization?
- Did the organization ever use the plan?
- Does anyone remember anything about the old plan?

If the answer is *no* to these questions, then the next question is, do you want to go down that same road again?

According to Robert S. Kaplan of the Balance Scorecard approach:

- 85% of management teams spend less than one hour a month on strategy issues.
- Only 27% of a typical company's employees have access to its Strategic Plan.
- 60% of typical organizations do not link their strategic priorities to their budget.
- 90% of well-formulated strategies fail due to poor execution.

These statistics are a sad commentary on Strategic Planning. Why bother with planning if it is doomed to fail?

If your organization has never had a Strategic Plan, the questions change. Do you want a plan that:

- really works?
- stays current?
- drives the organization?
- delivers success?

You're reading this book because you want to succeed in Strategic Planning. Other Strategic Planning approaches have left you confused. Understanding and implementing successful Strategic Planning is what Strategic Planning Demystified is all about.

< >

Strategic Planning Demystified

PART ONE
WHY STRATEGIC PLANS FAIL

It is important to understand why Strategic Plans fail if you want to successfully plan. The fact that you are reading this book suggests that you're looking for a new way to accomplish a meaningful, beneficial, and successful Strategic Planning process to replace your old and forgotten plan. Or this is your first experience with Strategic Planning and you want to be successful the first time.

Let's look at the indicators that will tell you when a Strategic Plan may not be as successful as it should. Understanding failure is the flip side of understanding success. If your current Strategic Planning effort has not been successful and contains some of these factors, you will gain ideas on how to improve your planning approach. If you're new to Strategic Planning, you'll learn what to avoid.

A. Indicators of Failed Planning

Your current Strategic Planning document:

- Doesn't have any blemishes, creases, or marks on it, suggesting that it has never been touched or used.
- Is permanently bound preventing the document from being easily updated.
- Has not been updated since it was first published (out of date by years).
- The title includes a time period (e.g., Five-Year Plan).
- Contains no targeted results for the organization's customer. No measurements to indicate when the plan is succeeding.

Strategic Planning Demystified

- Contains a long, wordy, unclear, and ambiguous Mission Statement which no one can remember.

- Has a Mission Statement that is actually a Function Statement. (The difference will be explained later.)

- Contains a Vision Statement which is interchangeable with the Mission Statement. (The difference will be explained later.)

- Lacks clear and understandable Mission, Goals, Objectives, Strategies, and Performance Measures.

- Does not list current and future resource estimates (e.g., staff, costs, technology, production) that support the Goals, Objectives, and Strategies.

- Does not indicate who is accountable for achieving each Goal, Objective, and Strategy.

- Does not describe the ramifications of failure.

- Is identical to a previously dysfunctional and out-of-date plan.

- Is full of abstract, wordy, lofty buzz words, cliches, generalizations, etc., making it difficult for anyone to really understand.

- Contains Core Values. (The reason will be explained later too.)

- Has stove-piped the major activities/services into separate parts with no discussion of their interrelationship to the rest of the organization.

And finally, an ancient Chinese proverb says, "A book tightly shut is but a block of paper." Or said in modern terms, "A never-opened Strategic Planning document is just a dust collector." So, swipe your hand across the document and see how much dust has collected on it (assuming you can find your copy). What does that tell you?

Strategic Planning Demystified

Your organization's Strategic Planning process:

- Has no ongoing Strategic Planning.
- Rarely reviews or updates the plan.
- Has the budget or fiscal calendar drive the process instead of influencing it. (There is a big difference between driving and influencing.)
- Has no connection or reference to other organizational plans (e.g., Business Plan, Technology Plan, Tactical Plan).
- Does not include stakeholder or customer input.
- Does not include or support all organizational components.
- Is unknown to most employees who can't recite or even paraphrase the Mission Statement.
- Is never part of management or executive meetings.
- Has no one managing the Strategic Plan on a continuing basis.

Indicators of poor planning management is when managers:

- Do not use the Strategic Plan.
- Have left no fingerprints on the planning document.
- Think that their Function is the Mission.
- Are not held accountable for their part of the plan.
- Do not keep the plan on or near their desk.
- Need the office secretary to find their copy of the plan.
- Set planning milestones to correspond with personnel review or fiscal cycles.
- Do not connect personnel review, performance, or appraisal elements to the plan's Goals or Objectives.

Strategic Planning Demystified

- Never take the plan to executive or management meetings.
- Believe that once the plan is completed, planning is done.
- Secretly consider the plan a waste of time.

In some cases, an organization may resist planning because managers:

- Fear a loss of control.
- Believe that looking into the future brings uncertainty.
- Fear that the planning effort will question competency.
- Believe that planning will require more work.
- Believe that planning will disrupt current work processes.
- Would rather have a colonoscopy, root canal, IRS audit, or file for bankruptcy than to conduct Strategic Planning.

Ultimately, Strategic Plans fail for the following reasons:

- Management thinks that the plan will help the staff, and staff thinks that the plan will help management, resulting in no one using the plan.
- The planning document is considered the end product to Strategic Planning. The strongest indicator to failed Strategic Planning is when an organization thinks that Strategic Planning has been successfully accomplished upon publishing the planning document.

Words of Wisdom About Strategic Planning:

- **The Strategic Planning document is a byproduct of planning, not the end product.**
- **You can have a successful Strategic Planning process without a document, but having a Strategic Planning document doesn't mean you have a successful Strategic Planning process.**

Understand, the Strategic Planning document is important. It outlines and documents the actions to be taken and who will be responsible for those actions. We place agreements, contracts, and plans in writing so that everyone understands their roles and responsibilities. The planning document, however, is not the end product! A good Strategic Planning document changes over time.

B. Committees

Most organizations form a Strategic Planning committee consisting of representatives from various components or departments. This suggests a democratic process where everyone has equal input. That is why it takes so long to create a plan. After lengthy discussions, a consensus takes place. As long as one component does not intrude upon another component, they usually agree on each other's Goals and Objectives. This results in a stove-piped document where each program is looked at separately with no real connection to the overall organization or to the customer. The plan is watered down to protect each other's turf or to simply play it safe. The committee will most likely settle for the most basic consensus. Once the plan is published, the committee is disbanded and the Strategic Planning process ends.

I strongly recommend not using a committee to formulate a Strategic Plan but instead use a trained planning facilitator. This position and how to approach planning will be discussed in greater detail later. What is important to know now is that the facilitator can evaluate each component's Goals/Objectives, etc., to ensure they support the broader organization's Goals and Objectives.

C. Planning Is Not Cyclical

> **Planning is linear.**

Many planning methods diagram the process showing it going round and round. You are expected to start over from the beginning. These images are confusing because each part appears to be equal in size and importance and you always come back to the beginning. The diagrams imply that the Strategic Planning process repeats the entire process over and over again. The following example diagrams show traditional planning charts.

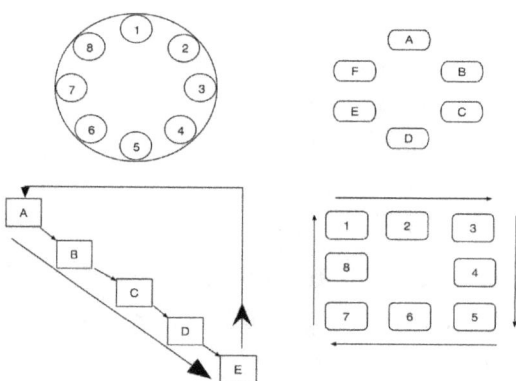

Planning is not cyclical, it is linear! Once you have identified your Mission, Goals, etc., you head for the horizon. Mission, Goals, Objectives, or other elements should be updated as changes occur to the business, technology, economy, social environment, customer requirements, etc. Linear planning forces an organization to pay constant attention to the plan. Whereas, cyclical planning suggests that you start over at some arbitrary point in the future. This results in people ignoring the plan until the next cycle, at which point the plan is out of date and requires a new plan.

Plan Today ↓

   Change Occurs in the Future ↓

      Update the Plan

Strategic Planning generally fails or falls short of success as a result of an organization's failure to recognize that planning is an ongoing organizational activity and not a single, infrequent, one-night stand. Weak or incorrect projections, assumptions, and predictions of the future cannot be avoided. That is why an ongoing analysis is crucial. As an organization moves into the future, incorrect assumptions begin to emerge. The earlier an organization identifies changing realities, the sooner the organization can adapt or change. And that change should be reflected in the Strategic Plan as it is updated.

D. Arbitrary Time Periods

Good Strategic Planning is an ongoing monitoring process that tracks the health of the organization in real time to ensure that the organization achieves its Mission and Goals. If you're feeling poorly, you don't wait for an annual checkup to decide what to do because by then, it could be too late. Although organizations usually react when an event occurs, the Strategic Plan, unfortunately, is usually not part of the change process and quickly becomes obsolete and outdated.

Imagine meeting your contractor for the first time to discuss your desire to build a family home. If the contractor's first words are, "Let's draw up a two year building plan," you would probably ask the contractor, "Why two years?" How can the contractor select a two-year time frame when you haven't told the contractor what kind of house you want, where it will be located, what your requirements are, or what resources you have. And yet, organizations start planning with an artificial time period based upon nothing. They do it all the time.

Strategic Planning Demystified

Many plans start as a "Five-Year Plan." Why five years? It is one of the first critical planning mistakes organizations make. How can you state "five years" without knowing the activities, time, and resources needed to accomplish the long-term Goals which you have not yet identified? I suspect organizations start out with a 'Five-Year Plan" because:

- It feels safe.
- It forces people to look beyond what they are doing today.
- It goes so far into the future that no one will be held accountable.
- Management hopes to be somewhere else in five years.
- Everyone else does it this way.

I recently saw references to "Ten-Year Plans." Who can plan ten years? A ten-year plan guarantees that no one will ever pay attention to the plan. An organization will be lucky if anyone even remembers it had a ten-year plan before the end of the ten years.

Don't get this confused with a long-term Project Plan (e.g., building an aircraft carrier or a sky scraper which could easily require ten years). Project-planning activities use sound planning methodologies with actual activity, schedule, and cost items. Once a Project Plan is developed, it is not unusual to make changes during its lifecycle and in fact, it is expected that changes will occur.

A good Strategic Plan outlines future efforts based upon the most up-to-date information and reasonable analysis. The planning timeline comes from an actual assessment into the effort needed to achieve the Mission, Goal, and Objective. Conducting a real analysis provides a more realistic and accurate timeline. A real planning process reduces the risk of failure because it is based on real analysis and assessments, and on the best available and educated assumptions.

As you move into the future, your plan moves forward into the future too and changes as required. So, your plan should never say "Five-Year Plan" because your planning document will never be finished but will be an ongoing and frequently updated plan. What happens in one or two years when you need to add or drop a Goal? Are you really going to wait five years to make changes? Simply title your planning document, "The Strategic Plan." You might add "updated on ##/##/####" on the cover page to show when the plan was last updated. Don't forget to put the Strategic Plan into a three-ring binder so you can change the plan when needed. If it has been years since the last update, that should also tell you something really important about the plan. "It isn't working!"

Good Strategic Planning holds the organization together like the human skeleton, giving support and attachment to the entire body. It becomes an integral part of the body. Whereas the typical five-year plan is like a suit of clothes tailored to your body but then hung in the closet. Five years later, you take it out and find it needs to be altered. You alter it and then back in the closet it goes, never to be seen or worn.

In some cases, an organization will be required by the government, funding source, or other management to create a five-year plan. Although the rules specify a five-year span, I would not let the requirement drive the analysis. If your analysis can go out 82 months, then put that into your plan. If you can't plan further than 42 months, then just cover the 42 months and explain why you can't project beyond the 42 months.

E. Timeline Mistakes

Another organizational planning problem occurs when Goals and Objectives are confined by fiscal or calendar years. This can result in squeezing in or stretching out the Goals and Objectives to fit into artificial, fixed timelines with no real basis. If a component is asked to list the activities it plans to conduct over the next four fiscal or calendar years, they may skip the analysis of how long it will actually take.

Chart 1 below shows the typical timeline where components are asked what fiscal year they plan to accomplish a Goal or Objective. Planning is easy because components believe no one will ever use this chart to follow their activities. The chart doesn't allow for a more precise projection. I can see the staff sitting around a table and saying, "It might take a year or two so let's just say it will take two years. Wow, that was easy." Without a true analysis, it might take one or three years. It is no wonder that organizations experience cost and schedule overruns.

Chart 1 - Fixed Timeline by Fiscal Year (FY)

	FY 1	FY 2	FY 3	FY 4
Upgrade	■	■	■	
Staff Hires	■	■	■	■
New Facility	■			
Connectivity	■	■		

Chart 2 shows how the same Objectives would look when a component is asked for an honest and educated analysis of the effort and resources needed to accomplish their Objectives without pre-set, artificial constraints. A component will have to conduct a difficult but real analysis which will result in a more accurate and meaningful plan. The "Upgrade" category (first row) shows that the project will begin in about

Strategic Planning Demystified

8 months and will require 22 months to finish. It clearly indicates that a real analysis has been conducted and forms the basis and justification for budget requests.

Chart 2 - Analysis-Based Timeline

	6 month	12 month	18 month	24 month	30 month	36 month	42 month
Upgrade		22 months	22 months	22 months			
Staff Hires	22 months	22 months	22 months		9 months	9 months	
New Facility	9 months						
Connectivity		18 months	18 months	18 months			

In **Chart 3**, the organization can overlay fiscal- or calendar-year grids to see how fiscal funding may influence the projects.

Chart 3 - Fiscal Year Relation to Analysis

	6 month	12 month	18 month	24 month	30 month	36 month	42 month
Fiscal Years	FY 1	FY 1	FY 2	FY 2	FY 3	FY 3	FY 4
Upgrade		22 months	22 months	22 months			
Staff Hires	22 months	22 months	22 months		9 months	9 months	
New Facility	9 months						
Connectivity		18 months	18 months	18 months			

Other considerations:

- Arbitrary time periods confine the staff to that time period. A subjective time period is an immediate constraint to a true analysis. An unconstrained, thorough, reasonable, and educated analysis must first be conducted to determine the actual activities, schedules, and resources that are needed to accomplish the organization's Goals and Objectives.

- Real Strategic Planning is never ending unless the organization ceases to exist. You should not start a new plan unless a major change or overhaul is needed for the Goals and Objectives. As time moves along, the plan will be updated as reality begins to influence the original analysis and assumptions.

- Another aspect of conducting an analysis is the negotiations that take place between managers. With an initial analysis laid out before management, decisions on funding and resources can be discussed. It is at this point that funding can influence the plan but the strength of a good analysis can push back to justify the required activities, schedules, and resources.

- Understand that when looking into the future by many years, target dates can be indicated by the year or, at best, quarter years, (e.g., fully automate process in the fourth year or the third quarter of the fourth year). You don't want to put a specific date for an event scheduled three or more years into the future. As these long-term targets become short-term Goals and Objectives (one or two years into the future), the target dates should become more precise, (e.g., complete Phase I in the 14th month or complete staff hiring by the 6th month).

- Important dates or numbers should be based on a true analysis and not pulled out of thin air. I found some staffs would select the last month of the fiscal year. This clearly indicated to me that they had not conducted an analysis. They had no clue how long the project was going to take so they played it safe.

F. Vision Versus Mission

> **A Vision Statement is not part of the planning process.**

The French writer Antoine de Saint-Exupery once said, "A goal without a plan is just a wish."

I define a Vision Statement as, "**A desired but not yet attainable end result for the customer.**" Vision is an idealistic, abstract, visionary statement, a wish or daydream. It is usually a one-time future event. Eliminate diabetes. Bring world peace. Manufacture the best consumer-desired widget on the planet. A Vision is something that you currently cannot create a plan to accomplish. You can't get there (Vision) from here. If you can accomplish the Vision, then the Vision is actually a Mission.

For example, the United Nations could have a Vision to "eliminate war, poverty, illiteracy, etc." This is a desired but not yet attainable end-result for the world (customer). It is an idealistic visionary statement. Whereas, a Mission Statement would be to "**reduce** war, poverty, illiteracy, etc.," results that can be planned and accomplished. Therefore, I strongly suggest that you leave the Vision Statement out of the planning process. A Vision Statement is okay for public relations or to build internal morale, but you really can't create a plan that will accomplish a Vision.

When National Aeronautical and Space Administration (NASA) scientists discuss the possibility of sending people to Mars, that would be a Vision. When NASA begins to apply resources to send someone to Mars, then going to Mars becomes a Mission.

Many times people will define a Vision Statement the way others define Mission. This results in confusion and a weak or Function-type Mission Statement and is followed by Function Goals, Objectives, etc. Function Goals lead to measuring internal Functions and not customer results. Focusing on Function is much easier but leads to a false sense of accomplishment. An organization that concentrates solely on Function blindly goes into the future.

For example, a diabetes foundation has a Vision to reduce diabetes. To support the Vision, the foundation creates a Mission to educate people on the dangers of diabetes. The Goals, Objectives, and Strategies then focus on educating people. This can result in a false sense of accomplishment by measuring only the successful educational activities (pamphlets distributed, public service announcements broadcasted, presentations made, etc.) while failing the Vision to reduce the incidents of diabetes.

It is no wonder organizations get confused about Strategic Planning. The following Mission and Vision definitions demonstrate the conflicting and confusing definitions found on the Internet.

Mission:

- Core purpose of an organization
- Answers the question, "What do we do?"
- Why it exists, and what it does to achieve its Vision
- "How" you plan to reach your Vision
- Mission comes first, followed by Vision
- Makes the Vision a reality
- Determines an organization's resources allocation

Strategic Planning Demystified

- The ultimate criteria against which actions and plans are measured
- Action Plan that drives the organization to accomplish the Vision
- Captures the uniqueness of your company and guides your quality and service
- Core purpose, identity, values, and principle business aims
- Managing with greatness and untamed strength, improving everything daily
- Will churn out revolutionary ideas about the mundane, banishing mediocrity

Vision:

- "What" an organization wants to accomplish
- Defines "what" the business will do and "why" it will exist tomorrow
- "Where" you want to be
- Points the direction of "where" the organization wishes to go
- Captures "what" achieving the Mission "looks like"
- Shorter-term horizon that guides strategic decision-making
- How the organization would like the world to be in which it operates
- Statement with three-decade horizons
- How the organization will look in the future
- Core set of principles that the company stands for
- Broad set of compelling criteria that will define organizational success
- Announces the organization's Goals and purpose to its employees, suppliers, customers, vendors, and the media
- Creates that momentum of growing anticipation about the future

Confused? You bet. Notice how the same words describe both Mission and Vision with the words "what, how, and why." They are vague and can be interpreted in many different ways. You will notice that some believe Mission comes before Vision and others believe Vision comes before Mission. Some use inspirational and lofty words while others use short generic words. People involved in planning for the first time face a myriad of vague definitions. Also note that very few of the Mission or Vision Statements mention a customer. How can you envision the future without including the customer?

Finally, notice how most definitions state that Mission and Vision are future events? Why would we have two words to be interchangeable when addressing the same future events? Future events needed to be redefined into two categories: 1) what I wish to achieve someday (Vision) and what I can achieve (Mission). I have given Mission and Vision their own unique definition to be logical and understandable to everyone. My short and clear definitions demystifies these statements. Here are my definitions:

Mission Statement: A desirable and attainable end result for the customer.

Vision Statement: A desired but not yet attainable end result for the customer.

Understanding this difference between Mission and Vision is critical to your planning. If your Mission Statement focuses on your customer, you improve your chances of a successful planning process. After years of experience, I concluded that a Vision Statement does not belong in the planning process.

For more examples showing the confusion between Mission and Vision Statements, read Appendix B.

G. Core Values

> **How the organization treats its customers and itself.**

Core Values are another traditional element that people inject into planning. These values, however, are not really part of planning. Core Values describe how the organization values and treats customers, suppliers, stakeholders, and the organization itself. Keywords used in Core Values are:

Accountability, ambition, civic responsibility, collaboration, commitment, compassion, competency, consistency, courage, credibility, customer service, dedication, dependability, dignity, diversity, efficiency, empowerment, fairness, flexibility, honesty, industriousness, innovation, integrity, justice, leadership, loyalty, optimism, ownership, passion, persistence, personal development, professionalism, recognition, respect, responsibility, safety, service excellence, teamwork, and trust.

Varying opinions exist on what is actually a Core Value. The point I'm making is - listing them in your plan is not planning. It may be true that Core Values define the organization's culture but it has little to do with planning. Core Values usually deal with office behavior and the philosophy for dealing with customers. Organizations use these values as a public relations tool to declare honesty, integrity, great customer service, etc., to create trust with the customers and employees. All organizations will claim to have positive Core Values whether true or not. What organization would admit to being lazy, dishonest, and inefficient? If an organization, however, requires a Goal or Objective to achieve a positive Core Value, well, that may not be a good sign. Is your organization full of corrupt, incompetent, lazy, dishonest, inflexible people building or selling such defective products that you need a Goal or Objective to improve the organization's Core Values? Let's hope not.

    Listing a Core Value(s) in the Mission Statement (e.g., be an honest organization) could suggest a negative. If an organization needs a Core Value of honesty in the future, what does that say about the organization today? Be careful in listing a Core Value in the Mission Statement and only if it's absolutely necessary. One exception could be a Mission to maintain what could be construed as a Core Value (e.g., continue to provide the highest level of honest service).

    Another exception could be the need to address a weak Core Value in order to improve the organization's effectiveness and the integrity of products available to customers. Only then, however, should a Core Value be included in the planning process. For example, an increase in returned defective products may require an Objective or Strategy to improve workers' attention to manufacturing quality. At this point, a poorly performing Core Value becomes a risk factor that needs to be addressed within the plan.

    Another exception would be where a new company wants to hire new employees who meet a set of Core Values. A Core Value could be an Objective that addresses the type of employees to be hired.

    A Core Value, in some instances, can be a Goal, Objective, or Strategy. Hopefully, the plan is to maintain a Core Value rather than working to achieve one. If you wish to cite your Core Values in a planning document, fine, but there should be a good reason. A plan that simply lists Core Values is just useless rhetoric that burdens the reader.

    One last point. The customer's opinion of the product or service actually represents the front-end of Core Values. Products that meet or exceed customer expectations for high quality, honest values, etc., can only exist when the internal Core Values are focused on high quality, honest values, etc., for the customer. Said another way, the end-products reflect an organization's internal Core Values. Customers only care about the end-product that they receive. If the product is poor, then they will believe the organization's values are poor too. If the product is marvelous, then the organization is seen as being marvelous.

H. Poor Executive Management

> Poor management can hurt planning.

Some executives or managers will defeat good planning. There are several types of managers that would make any good planning effort difficult to initiate or succeed.

- Status Quo Manager: Don't rock the boat and don't change anything because change has risks.

- Short-Timer Manager: Waiting for a better position to become available and has little or no commitment to improving the organization.

- Denial Manager: Unreceptive to bad news, thus inhibiting staff from warning of potential problems; an optimist who believes that things will work out; doesn't get stressed over details; and believes that the organization is okay.

- Weak or Lethargic Manager: Does not have the energy or initiative to make changes and is not receptive to change.

- Empire Manager: So fearful of losing power that the manager will throw roadblocks to stop change or refuse to cooperate in order to protect his/her empire.

- New Manager: Just arrived, has no clue what's going on, and is hesitant to take any action.

- Function Manager: Focuses on Function and not on results.

- Micro Manager: Manages each detail, over supervising, getting so involved in projects that project managers can't manage their responsibilities and Goals.

- Complex Manager: Creates complicated and convoluted plans and projects that can't be adequately tracked for success or performance.

- Deaf Manager: Won't listen to employees or other managers, and when the manager does listen, does nothing with the information.

- Over-commitment Manager: Promises results that have not been planned and cannot be accomplished, and without first consulting with the department that will get stuck trying to meet the manager's over-extended promises.

The above managers consider planning a waste of time because they never had the experience of using good planning in the past and may be too set in their ways to change now. They see planning as something for someone else to do. I'm mentioning these negative managers because if you work for one of these managers, it will be difficult to initiate a good Strategic Planning process. If you are one of the managers described above, you need to change.

For an executive who has a subordinate manager who fits in one of the above categories, take the manager aside and assure him/her that good Strategic Planning will be good for his/her career. Good planning improves performance. A strong executive should be able to nurture and improve a poor performing manager. It is crucial that you have energized, end-result oriented, performance-based managers for Strategic Planning.

Strategic Planning Demystified

A manager below an ineffective manager can, however, still implement Strategic Planning Demystified at his/her own level. Good Strategic Planning can be implemented at any level. So read on and learn how you can successfully plan for those activities that you have control to change and improve, even if the manager above you does not understand good Strategic Planning.

SUMMARY: Traditional Strategic Planning methodologies usually fail because.

- The current Strategic Planning document is not used.
- There is no ongoing planning process.
- Managers are not using the plan.
- Organizations resist planning.
- Committees produce weak plans.
- The plan is cyclical.
- Arbitrary time periods constrain the plan.
- Calendar timelines drive planning.
- Plan contains confusing Vision and Mission Statements.
- Planning definitions are ambiguous.
- List of Core Values provide no value.
- Poor executive management.

< >

Strategic Planning Demystified

PART TWO
STRATEGIC PLANNING DEMYSTIFIED

Strategic Planning Demystified offers a better approach to planning. It is a lean, mean, planning machine that works. It offers a simple and straight forward approach. In addition, the wheel has not been reinvented here. The wheel has been upgraded from nylon bias to steel-belted radials to keep you on the road and improve your ability to reach your destination.

Strategic Planning Demystified provides the following benefits:

- A solid, down-to-earth, structured planning approach.

- A follow-through process with clear beginnings and endings based on reality.

- A planning solution that answers the question, where can we take the customer?

- An ongoing, active, and usable planning process. Rather than a one-night stand, the planning process remains up-to-date as the organization moves into the future. A planning blueprint that changes when required.

- A planning approach that focuses on reality.
  - Rather than starting with artificial time periods, the process identifies what can and needs to be accomplished with a reasonable estimate of the required activities, schedules, and resources.
  - Conducts a real analysis so that all milestones and timelines have a basis in reality. Good planning keeps an organization on schedule and budget, reduces the waste of resources, and improves the delivery of products to the customer.

- Stays up-to-date in real-time, not impeded by fixed scheduled updates and reviews that are unrelated to ongoing events. The plan changes when it needs to be changed. (Do you notice a reoccurring theme here?)
- Recognizes that forecasts about the future contain imperfect data. As the future becomes the present, an organization can update the imperfect data with the new, accurate data that has arrived.
- Organization's resources can be tracked to a plan's Goals, Objectives, and Strategies.

- Recognizes that processes and expectations change over time and that a planning process must be resilient and flexible. Imagine a football team waiting to evaluate the game strategy at half time rather than when it becomes apparent the team is losing. The team needs to change strategies now, not wait for some artificially set time period. As in football, when you realize you're falling behind, you call a time-out to regroup, analyze the problem, change or update the game plan, and return to the field with a new invigorated Strategy.
- Integrates with Tactical or other organizational plans. Most Strategic Plans fail to make any connection to Tactical/Action/Business Plans. How can an organization achieve long-term Goals without a short-term Tactical, Action, or Business Plan?
- Clearly defines and interconnects Mission, Goals, Objectives, and Strategies throughout the organization. All major components must have their own set of Mission, Goals, etc., which eventually support the organization's overall Mission, Goals, Objectives, and Strategies.
- Holds management accountable for performance, both individually and organizationally. Traditional plans rarely list who will be responsible for accomplishing each part of the plan. The Strategic Planning Demystified approach lists the organizational title of the person responsible for each Goal, Objective, and Strategy. This

makes managers accountable for their parts of the plan and requires them to report changes when they occur. It forces them to pay attention to the plan.

- PRMs (Performance and Result Measurements) that track success and identify potential risks or failures. Identifying and tracking key Performance Measures helps to validate that Goals and Objectives are being accomplished or that they need to be adjusted.

- Provides employees with the knowledge of where they belong within the plan. Each employee should be able to see how their Function supports the organization. A good plan requires that each employee's job description points to one of the organization's or component's planning Goal, Objective, and/or Strategy. This includes personnel in administrative, housekeeping, facility management, etc. All employee Functions support the organization and can be found within the plan, either directly, indirectly, generally, or implied. Being accountable also pressures and inspires employees with less initiative and work ethic to strive for success.

- Empowers staff to achieve success for actions which they control and can change. When employees have a clearly defined and achievable Mission, Goal, Objective, and Strategies, they have a strong incentive to succeed.

- Improves morale by focusing employees on success and not Function. When employees understand their positive contribution to the organization's or customer's success, they become energized to succeed.

- Validates the current organizational structure or discloses organizational misalignment.

- Prevents Mission creep by requiring that any proposed new task or activity must support the Strategic Plan.

- Gives all employees a clear understanding of the Mission.
- Reduces complacency.
- Improves positive attitude and commitment towards planning.
- Produces better planning decisions which reduces the tendency to constantly and arbitrarily change priorities.
- Maintains continuity for new mangers.
- Becomes an integral part at all major meetings.
- Helps to accurately predict what is going to happen in the near future; detect important trends; and keep minds open to new possibilities.
- Provides a good analysis at both what you know and what you need to know.

Four key elements to Planning

Planning requires the presence of four critical key elements for successful planning. If one or more of these elements is not in place, the planning effort may not be fully successful. They are briefly described here but a detailed explanation follows.

1) **Executive Commitment:** Without senior or executive management's strong commitment to the Strategic Planning process, no Strategic Plan will be successful! Leadership comes from the organization's President, Chief Executive Officer, Director, etc. Leadership needs to demand full compliance throughout the organization and will back up his/her commitment to the planning process.

2) **Mission Statement:** The right Mission Statement is crucial to a successful plan. A vague or Function Statement leads to weak and Function-type Goals, Objectives, etc. A Mission Statement must be

on target. A great Mission Statement will produce performance- and result-oriented Goals, Objectives, and Strategies.

3) **PRMs:** An organization must measure the affect of its end product on the customer. How can an organization know if it is being successful without measuring the customer's success with the product? Using only Function measurements (e.g., how many widgets sold or how many pamphlets distributed) can lead to a false sense of short-term success, while eventually failing the customer. Good PRMs substantiate and validate an organization's value to the customer.

4) **Accountability to the Plan:** Management and staff need to stay focused on achieving the Strategic Plan. When all employees are held accountable for what they control and influence in the plan, the plan becomes useful and productive. This can be accomplished by either a separate contract or by including the planning Goals and Objectives into existing personnel performance or rating reports. Ultimately, accountability leads to clarity as to the results that a manager and staff need to accomplish.

In looking at these four requirements, they can be paired into two important parts.

1) **Managing the Organization:** Executive Commitment and Accountability represent the management of the organization. The organization's top leadership holds managers and employees accountable for accomplishing the plan's Goals and Objectives.

2) **Managing the Product:** The Mission and its PRMs focus the organization on managing and delivering a product that meets or exceeds the customers' requirements.

SUMMARY: Strategic Planning Demystified provides an opportunity to create a planning approach that works. Many organizations create traditional Strategic Plans but end up with a failed approach. Good leadership starts and maintains the process. Holding managers accountable promotes an ongoing planning process. Having the right Mission Statement brings all other planning elements into their correct supporting roles. Measuring the impact on the customer produces the evidence of whether the planning process is proceeding as planned or not.

PART THREE
STRATEGIC PLANNING

Strategic Planning Demystified contains eight components needed for successful planning. When you finish reading this part, you'll have a clear understanding of how to create a successful Strategic Plan.

The basis for my Strategic Planning approach comes from the Government Performance and Results Act of 1993 (GPRA), U.S. Public Law 103-62. Background on GPRA can be found in Appendix C. GPRA provides a logical, organized, results-oriented planning approach that seeks positive results from organizations. The GPRA contains the basic elements found in most Strategic Planning approaches and can be adapted to any organization. For good reason, Vision Statement and Core Values were left out of the GPRA, and as previously stated, I have left these two items out of my planning approach too. I've modified, however, the GPRA definitions to be more results oriented.

The eight major components for a successful Strategic Planning process:

1. Executive Commitment
2. Mission Statement
3. Goal
4. Objective
5. Strategy
6. PRMs
7. Accountability
8. Analysis

A. Executive Commitment

> **Strategic Planning needs strong leadership and commitment.**

A successful planning process must have strong leadership and a commitment at the highest level of the organization. An executive starts by asking:

- What product do we provide our customer?
- What does our customer do with our product?
- Are we meeting our customer's needs?
- Are we satisfied at what our organization is doing for our customer?
- Where can we take our customer?
- What does the organization need to do to meet our customers' needs in the future?

Leadership must demand a successful planning process. The following phrases best describe executive commitment:

- agency or company director, president, CEO, etc., wants successful planning to happen
- demands an innovative, useful, beneficial, and successful results-oriented planning process
- emotionally fired up, excited, eager, passionate, committed, and down right fanatical about having the correct planning process
- understands and appreciates the value of good Strategic Planning
- demands and commands that all levels of the organization get on board with planning

- appoints a Strategic Planning Coordinator (SPC) at the executive level, further stressing the importance placed by leadership in this effort
- makes the planning process an integral part of all major meetings at all levels of the organization
- holds each manager accountable for his/her part of the plan
- motivated because past efforts have been less than successful

I have observed that when leadership paid attention to the Strategic Plan's Goals and Objectives, the Strategic Planning process worked. When leadership simply tells the organization, "Here is your plan," and pays little attention to it, the plan dies. When supervisors and employees see that leadership is not using the plan, they ignore it too.

With the help of a trained SPC, the Strategic Planning process begins with the most senior executive defining the Mission Statement. Later in the process, the lower level managers will use the Mission Statement to formulate and submit the organization's Goals and Objectives for the executive's approval. This process will be explained in Part Eight.

B. Mission Statement

> **A desirable and attainable end result for the customer.**

The Mission Statement describes the organization's current or future impact on the customer by the organization's product. Starting with the correct Mission Statement, an organization can lay out a plan that will achieve the Mission. A good, strong Mission Statement forces the Goals, Objectives, and Strategies to stay focused on actions that will accomplish the Mission. A customer-focused Mission will result in an organization's success.

A clearly defined, customer-performance-based Mission Statement will inspire and excite the organization to grasp and embrace the Mission. With the right Mission Statement on the front door or at the top page of the organization's publications, customers will know that the organization will strive to meet or exceed their expectations. Employees will be excited and eager to meet the Mission's challenge when producing or delivering the product to the customer.

The Mission Statement is what:

- Must be accomplished for the customer.
- The customer accomplishes using the product.
- Is most important to the customer.
- Defines success for the organization.
- The customer describes as the Mission.

Mission Statement must:

- Be right on target.
- Clearly define what needs to be accomplished.
- Contain an explicit or implied win or fail proposition.
- Be challenging.
- Be measurable for success.

Creating a Mission Statement:

> **The core of the Mission Statement (customer benefit) should be stated within the first ten words.**

Describe the customer benefit at the beginning of the statement so that both the organization and the customer can clearly understand and remember what the organization is trying to accomplish. Burying the essence of the Mission Statement in the middle or end of the statement weakens the statement and appears secondary to the Function Statements made in the beginning.

When evaluating the Mission Statement, ask these questions:

For a Business:

- What will the product accomplish for the customer?
- What will the customer accomplish with the product?
- What is the customer expecting for their money?

For a Non-Profit Agency:

- What will the services accomplish for the client or patient?
- What result does the client or patient expect to receive?
- What result do the stakeholders (contributors/supporters/sponsors) expect for their donations?

For a Government Agency:

- What does the taxpayer get for their taxes?
- What result does the taxpayer expect for their taxes?
- What result is expected by legislation, regulations, etc.?

Mission Statement Description: The Mission Statement can have one or more results-oriented statements. The Mission Statement should be short (ten words or less) and may be followed with optional statements that further describe what will be done, for whom, and with what.

- **Core Component:** Accomplish something positive and measurable for the customer (better service, enjoyable experience, delicious meal, long-term reliability, meet or exceed customer requirements, reduce disease, save lives, improve effectiveness, reduce poverty, reduce pollution, etc.).

- **Optional Components:** A list of supporting descriptors.
  - By doing something (delivery of a quality, timely, and/or affordable product)
  - For someone (customer, consumer, taxpayer, client, patient, community, etc.)
  - With something (product, education, training, research, etc.)

What to consider when creating the Mission Statement:

- The core Mission Statement should be short enough so that employees and customers can remember it or can accurately paraphrase it.

- A Mission may be to improve the customer's experience sometime in the future (increase productivity, improve health, etc.) or maintain a critical level of service today (e.g., maintain timely service, continue to deliver quality meals, continue building safe cars, maintain health, retain a clean environment).

- The Mission Statement can change when the Mission changes or is achieved.

- A good Mission is usually difficult to achieve but has a significant positive end result. If the Mission is easy to accomplish and hard to fail, then it is a weak Mission, or worse, a Function Statement (e.g., sell meals, deliver packages, repair cars, educate students, manage store.)

- A Mission should be held to a significant standard or measurement for success (what the customer would consider success).

- A Mission Statement can have more than one Mission within the statement but should be highlighted in bullets to clearly outline the different Mission Statements.

- A Mission should not be buried in a long and wordy paragraph(s).

- Mid- and lower-level organizational Mission Statements can be a one-time but crucial activity (e.g., fully automate the inventory system or expand marketing into the Internet) or maintaining an ongoing level of performance.

Mission Statements for similar organizations: Organizations of a similar nature can have similar Mission Statements. For example, the following organization categories can have a similar core Mission.

- **Law Enforcement:** Reduce criminal activity or make the community safer.

- **Education:** Help students achieve their vocation.

- Health: Improve or maintain patients' health.

- **Restaurant:** Provide an affordable, timely, and delicious dining experience that exceeds the customer's expectations.

- **Auto Repair Shop:** Repair cars that stay repaired at affordable prices and completed when promised.

- **Software Company:** Improve customer's productivity and performance with reliable and affordable business programs.

You can customize the Mission Statement by inserting a geographical location (e.g., citizens of Detroit), a specific level of performance (e.g., reduce diabetes disease), or by inserting the organization's name (e.g., customers of ABC Computer Store). Now look at these examples of customized Mission Statements.

- **Automotive Service:** Keep the customers' cars mechanically reliable and safe by providing affordable and professional maintenance services for their personal or business automobiles in the Detroit area.

- **Health Center:** Improve or stabilize diabetics' health by providing affordable, timely, and competent health care in the Richmond area.

- **State Law Enforcement Identification Bureau:** Reduce criminal activity in Virginia by providing law enforcement and civil agencies with timely, accurate, and relevant criminal identification services.

NOTE: Businesses exist to make money. You would think "making profit" would be a key Mission. If a business does not make profit, it's going to fail. Making money separates a business from non-profit and government organizations. As important as profit is for a business, however, it actually should not be the sole Mission. A Mission's real cornerstone is the customer who provides the profit. Without meeting the customer's satisfaction or requirements, you can initially make money but eventually fail if customers stop buying your product.

In fact, making money is so basic for a business, it is like saying that humans have the Mission to breathe. We don't, however, go through life saying our Mission is to breathe; it's too basic (unless you're in a submarine). Whereas, humans do have Missions to acquire food, clothing, shelter, companionship, etc. So a business's Mission should not be "to make money." You can, however, have a Goal or Objective addressing the need to make or increase profits that support the Mission.

Performance categories for various organizational Missions:

The following four performance categories can be used when wording your Mission. For example, take the word "improve" and place it in front of the subject, as in to improve quality or improve effectiveness. Another example would be the word "reduce," as in to reduce accidents or reduce defective parts. These words describe some measurable action that will benefit the customer.

- **Performance numbers go up** - Improve/increase/raise/expand something that benefits the customer, e.g., improve service.

- **Performance numbers go down** - Reduce/decrease/lower/prevent/avoid something that will benefit the customer, e.g., reduce defects.

- **New performance numbers** - Develop/achieve/initiate/open/create something new that benefits the customer, e.g., create new medical treatments.

- **Performance numbers remain the same** - Maintain/continue/sustain/provide a level of service for the customer, e.g., continue providing affordable care.

You may have other similar words that can be used when stating the Mission. These words can also be used when crafting Goal and Objective Statements. As you read the samples for Mission Statements below, identify the categories and words used to measure the action(s) to be taken for the customer.

Approaches to creating the Mission Statement: There are two approaches to creating a Mission Statement. The primary and best approach is taking the customer's point-of-view. What does the customer want or expect. A secondary approach comes from looking at the internal Function side of the organization. Both start with a series of questions. I prefer using the customer's point-of-view approach. Looking at Function is more common for government and non-profit organizations, whereas businesses are more accustom to using the customer approach.

Customer's point-of-view: Organizations deliver products to one or more categories of customer. Asking the following questions will help the organization identify what each customer group expects or needs to receive from the organization's product(s). Does the customer want to:

- Receive adequate, better, or best quality?
- Pay inexpensive, average, or premium cost?
- Receive average, reasonable, better, or exceptional delivery?
- Receive average, reasonable, better, or exceptional customer service?

What customer doesn't want the best quality service, lowest price, and work done in a timely manner? Doesn't matter if the customer is buying a car, getting a medical checkup, obtaining social welfare, receiving a cleaner environment, etc. Most customers, however, realize that there may be a tradeoff between quality, price, and timeliness. For example:

For-Profit: A greasy hamburger joint may provide inexpensive and timely service while serving a lower quality, less-healthy product.

Non-Profit: A medical clinic may provide low-income families with low-cost service by a qualified medical staff but with long waiting times.

Government: A law enforcement agency may be reducing crime within a short period of time but at a high financial cost.

An organization must ask itself: How can it meet the customer's requirements or expectations? Can it provide the lowest cost, highest quality, and quickest service? In most cases, you cannot but that does not mean your Mission can't be successful. Remember, the customer will drive the Mission. Determine what is most important to the customer and aim to deliver it. Most customers want an automobile tire store to install the best quality tire. Cost and timeliness would be second and third priority. Whereas, some people prefer inexpensive tires knowing its not the best quality but where cost is the most important factor. So, a tire company may focus on offering a selection of both top quality and affordable tires. The company is addressing customers that have different requirements.

Function Statement approach: Organizations are usually organized by Function: production, training, sales, administration, research, automation, etc. Producing or managing a product is a Function. Functions are part of the Tactical Plan but are not usually stated regarding the level of performance needed for achieving organizational-level Goals and Objectives. When planning, you can start with a Function Statement and ask: What is the final result or product performance to be achieved by conducting a Function? This is particularly helpful when trying to identify an administrative or supporting component's Mission. What Mission is the organization's Function trying to achieve?

Business Example:

    Example: Car dealer sells cars (Function).

        Question: What kind of cars do you sell?
        Answer: Cars that customers want to buy.

        Question: What kind of cars do customers want to buy?
        Answer: Cars that are reliable and affordable.

        Car Dealer's Mission Statement: Sell reliable and affordable cars.

Non-Profit Example:

    Example: Medical clinic conducts medical exams (Function).

        Question: Why does the clinic conduct medical exams?
        Answer: To identify patient's medical problem.

Question: Why does the clinic need to identify patient's medical problem?
Answer: To treat or cure the medical problem.

Question: Why does the clinic need to treat or cure the medical problem?
Answer: So that people may live long, healthy, and productive lives.

Medical Clinic's Mission Statement: Help people live longer and healthier lives through early identification and treatment of medical problems.

Example: Diabetes foundation educates people about the dangers of diabetes (Function).

Question: Why does the foundation need to educate people about diabetes?
Answer: To help people avoid diabetes.

Question: Why should people avoid diabetes?
Answer: Help people live long and healthy lives.

Diabetes Foundation's Mission Statement: Help people live healthy lives by avoiding diabetes.

The above two non-profit examples show how two different organizations can have a similar Mission Statement, "Help people live healthy lives." The medical clinic prevents diabetes or some other disease through medical examination. Whereas, the foundation prevents diabetes through education. The organization's unique action (e.g., medical exams) customizes the Mission Statement, distinguishing it from the other organization's Mission Statement (to educate).

Government Example:

Example: Law enforcement component conducts criminal background checks for day care agency applicants (Function).

Question: Why conduct criminal background checks?
Answer: To notify day care agencies if an applicant has a disqualifying criminal history record.

Question: Why notify day care agencies regarding a candidate's disqualifying criminal history record.
Answer: To ensure a disqualified candidate (e.g., pedophile) is not given access to children.

Question: Why keep a pedophile from children?
Answer: To keep children safe.

Law Enforcement Component Mission Statement: Keep children safe by reducing the incidents of sexual assault on children by checking applicant's background.

When the question seems to make sense but the answer seems to be unspecific, continue asking the "why" question. When the answer seems to make sense (protect children), and the next question seems illogical (e.g., why protect children), then the previous answer is probably the Mission Statement.

Another way of looking at the difference between Function and Mission would be the following statements:

Function	Mission
Deliver packages	Packages delivered in a timely and undamaged condition
Teach math	Improve students' math skills
Educate students	Help students achieve their vocation
Build highways	Build safe and effective highways
Educate about diabetes	Reduce incidences of diabetes
Build computers	Improve customers' productivity through technology
Provide defense counsel	Present the client's best case before the court
Manage the environment	Improve people's health by reducing air pollution

A Function Statement simply states an action or activity. Mission Statement states an outcome or result to be achieved and can be measured for success.

Point-of-Diminishing-Return Theory: When a Mission is to improve the product's quality, reduce the response time, or reach some targeted efficiency, it is assumed it is attainable. Once the efficiency is attained, the organization needs to determine if it can further improve performance. In some cases, the organization may have reached a point where further improvements would not provide a significant benefit to the customer. To lose what has been gained, however, would not be good. At that point, the Mission Statement can be changed to reflect an effort to *maintain* the current performance level for the customer.

There is a risk, however, that an organization will sit back, maintain a certain performance level, and fail to conduct ongoing analysis to identify potentially new approaches or improvements. Maintaining service runs the risk that competition or problems will overtake the organization, causing it to fail. When an organization achieves its Mission (e.g., timely response), it should consider modifying or adding a new Mission, such as improving quality, accuracy, or availability; expanding products, etc. This is another reason to have an ongoing analysis to detect possible changes in the customer's environment.

While some computer companies achieved success in building and selling desktop computers, some have failed by focusing on being a company that makes computers (Function) while failing to recognize changing customer requirements for smaller devices. Some companies became complacent and simply maintained current performance.

Mission Statement at different levels of the organization: At the top of a large organization, the Mission Statement is broad and general. It directly affects the customer(s). As you move lower into the organization, the Mission for each organizational component becomes more specific. These sub-Missions should support a Goal at the next higher level of the organization.

Chart 4 shows how this works. In this simple example, an organization has three planning levels: organization, mid-, and lower-level plans. The mid-level Mission Statement supports the Goal at the organization's level. The low-level Mission Statement supports the mid-level Goal. This process works at each level of the organization. In some cases, the mid-level Goal might also support one of the organization's Objectives.

Chart 4 - Mission Levels

Organization's Mission	Example of Multi-Layer Mission Statements		
Goal ↑	←Mid-Level Mission		
Objective ↑	← Goal ↑	←Lower-Level Mission	
Strategy ↑	← Objective ↑	← Goal ↑	
	Strategy ↑	← Objective ↑	
		Strategy ↑	

Look at the bones in your hand. Starting at the finger tips, the small bones connect to larger bones, resulting in a hand which then connects to the arms, etc. They all support the overall Mission to be able to grasp, hold, and/or throw an object. The group connection of lower organizational components impacts the organization's overall level of performance. The Strategic Planning process should clearly show an inter- connection where lower-level activities support higher-level activities.

The examples below show how one part of a Mission Statement tracks down through three levels of an organization to demonstrate how the subordinate Mission Statements would support the higher-level Mission Statement.

Business Example:

Mission: Provide quality vegetables at reasonable prices and deliver when promised.

Goal: Deliver products when promised or sooner.

> **Distribution Division's Mission:** Improve delivery time to customers.
>
> **Goal:** Improve availability of delivery trucks to meet or exceed delivery schedules.
>
>> **Transportation Section's Mission:** Ensure on-time deliveries by providing sufficient number of available trucks and drivers to meet delivery schedules.
>>
>> **Goal:** Meet delivery schedules by reducing truck downtimes and breakdowns by ensuring that all trucks meet rigid and comprehensive maintenance schedules.
>
> **Analysis:** At each organizational level, the Mission supports a Goal at the next highest level. This ensures that all organizational activities are connected. Each lower level activity supports a broader activity (Goal) at the higher level of the organization.

Non-Profit Example:

Mission: Restore vision and prevent blindness.

Goal: Acquire new treatments through research.

> **Research Division's Mission:** Restore vision by developing new treatments through advanced research techniques.
>
> **Goal:** Identify causes to sight-related children diseases by conducting neurological research studies.
>
>> **Child Research Unit's Mission:** Find treatments for children eye diseases caused by neurological disorders.
>>
>> **Goal:** Conduct research into neurons-produced complex cognitions and behaviors. Analysis suggests this research should

take 38 months to 42 months to identify relationship of neuron behaviors and juvenile eye disease.

Analysis: As with the other examples, an organization's lowest level has a Mission and Goal that support the next upper level in the organization. This ensures that all actions within an organization will directly or indirectly support the overall organization's Mission.

Government Example:

U.S. Department of Justice (DOJ) Mission: Provide Federal leadership in *preventing and controlling crime.*

DOJ Goal: *Prevent crime.*

FBI Mission: *Reduce crime* by providing criminal justice services to Federal, state, municipal, and international agencies and partners.

FBI Goal: *Reduce crime* by supporting Federal, state, local and international partners with identification and information services.

FBI CJIS Division Mission: *Reduce criminal and terrorist activities* by maximizing the ability to provide timely and relevant criminal justice information to the FBI and to qualified law enforcement, criminal justice, civilian, academic, employment, and licensing agencies concerning individuals, stolen property, criminal organizations and activities, and other law enforcement related data.

CJIS Goal: Provide law enforcement 24-hour uninterrupted access to the NCIC system.

Analysis: As you can see, each component's Mission supports a Goal above it. This maintains a strong focus throughout the organization for those components with the responsibility for providing leadership through criminal information services.

Strategic Planning Demystified

The CJIS Division Mission starts with a specific targeted performance Mission Statement indicating the end results for Americans (reduce crime). It is followed by describing its performance (timely and relevant information), its customers (FBI, law enforcement, civilian, etc.) and services (information on individuals, stolen property, etc.).

Recently, the CJIS Division changed the Mission Statement to the following: "**To equip our law enforcement, national security, and intelligence community partners with the criminal justice information they need to protect the United States while preserving civil liberties.**"

I believe it is a weak and watered down statement. The statement, "to equip" is a Function, not a Mission. It will lead to measuring outputs. It would be stronger if it stated, "**Provide relevant and valuable law enforcement information to our law enforcement, national security, and intelligence community partners to protect the United States while preserving civil liberties.**" Providing "**relevant and valuable law enforcement information**" will require outcome measurements to ensure that the information is protecting the United States. I've provided three versions. Which version do you think provides the best Mission Statement? Reduce crime, provide relevant and valuable information, or to equip?

SUMMARY: By now, you should understand that the Mission Statement is the crucial keystone to planning. It forms the portal to organizational success and improvement. The Mission must connect to the customer because the customer is why the organization exists. Supported by Goals, Objectives, Strategies, and PRMs, the Mission

Statement focuses and embraces the customer and guides the organization into the future. Disregard the customer at your own peril.

At an organization's lower-level, some components' customers may be other components within the organization. Examples might be components that provide office supplies, financial management, facility management, etc. Such components do not deal directly with the product to the customer but support the components that deal with the customer. As difficult as it is, these support components must also be connected to the Strategic Plan, either directly, indirectly, or implied.

APPENDIX A contains more examples of Mission Statements.

C. Goal

> **A major accomplishment or activity needed to reach or support the Mission.**

With a well-crafted Mission Statement in hand, now ask the question, what major event(s) or activity(ies) must be achieved or conducted to meet, approach, or support the Mission? An organization will most likely have several Goals that each address a major customer-related activity. All internal organization activities will support one or more of these top-level Goals. Each top-level Goal forms a contract between upper- and lower-level managers.

Goals also represent a form of measurement and progress indicator. Achieving each Goal provides an organization a reference point in its effort to achieve the Mission. That is, a Goal should be attaining, improving, or maintaining a certain performance level which can be measured. In some cases, the measurement identifies or reveals the Goal. If an organization experiences an increase in defective parts, that measurement may require a new Goal to reduce defective parts, improve quality, etc. If the organization discovers a new customer base, a Goal for increasing its customer base may be needed.

General descriptors that define a Goal at the top level of the organization:

- Describes a result that must be achieved to meet the Mission over time.
- Is worded like a Mission Statement.
- Gives substance to the Mission.
- Can be accomplished.
- Is a significant or major activity.
- Achieves or maintains a critical level of service for the customer.
- May accomplish a one-time but crucial event or activity.
- May be achieved in chronological order with or independent from other Goals.
- Can be measured for success.
- Can be stated as a level of performance.
- Should have the implied risk of failure.
- Is challenging but not impossible. If the Goal can be accomplished with very little effort, it may not be a Goal.
- Is a milestone that indicates if the organization is on track for success.
- Usually requires a significant time period (years) to accomplish for large organizations.
- Is modified or replaced with a new Goal once the Goal is either completed or found not relevant.

- Can be measured by output (products produced, production time, profit, cost, etc.) but the better measurement would be outcome (satisfied customers, reduction in disease, increase in customers, improved product reliability, achieving mandated legislative action, etc.) In most cases, the measurement is implied within the Goal Statement (e.g., increase customers, expand markets, improve health).
- May represent an effort to maintain a certain performance level, and therefore, rarely change.
- Describes a major and significant effort but is rarely an internal issue regarding management, function, process, or activity.
- Keeps the organization on track.
- Gives employees a strong sense of direction.

Accountability: Each Goal should list the manager's title where it can be easily seen. From herein, examples will include "(Manager Title)" to remind readers that someone needs to be cited as being responsible for the Goal, Objective, and Strategy.

Resource Requirements: Under each Goal, there should be a summary of the current and projected resources required for achieving or working towards the Goal. This resource summary consists of the cumulative resource totals from the Objectives supporting the Goal. Sometimes the numbers won't match with the lower numbers if some staff members or resources support more than one Objective. What is important is that an analysis has identified the required resources so that management has some idea of what it will take to achieve or work towards the Goal.

Requiring a resource list forces an organization to determine what actual actions must be taken. No more pie-in-sky estimates but a real analysis. It won't be easy. It will require real thinking to figure out what must be done and how it can be done.

As an organization moves into the future, these resource requirements will change as money is spent, progress is made on the schedule, staffing changes occur, etc. If everything is tracking as outlined in the resource section, then no changes to the plan should be necessary. If staff, cost, effort, and/or schedule significantly change, then updates to the Strategic Plan must be considered.

Small organizations should expect changes to occur frequently. Whereas, changes to large corporate plans will occur after a longer period of time. Said another way, it is the difference between changing direction in a canoe (small organization) because of a stiff breeze and changing direction in a super tanker (large organization). It takes a larger issue to change a large organization's direction. A new or startup organization is more sensitive to changes, and therefore, may need to change or modify its Goals over a shorter period of time.

You might be asking, who should do this analysis? It depends on the organization's size. Large corporations should already be analyzing this data. In some cases, particularly with mid- and large-sized organizations, an outside consultant may be needed with experience in using resource analysis tools, such as Activity Based Costing (described in Part Seven). Small and mid-sized companies may require an accountant or seasoned manager to track the data needed for the analysis. A small company's owner will be the most qualified person to identify the kind of assessment to be conducted. And of course, the sole-proprietor will be the person to conduct the analysis. With a start-up company, there will probably be only one or two measurements of value. The sole-proprietor will need to find the right measurement and a method of collecting at the point-of-sale to reduce the time and effort to collect data (e.g., survey customers when buying the product at the store).

Categories for various organizational Goals: Crafting a Goal Statement is similar to crafting a Mission Statement. The Goal describes a major activity to increase the positive, reduce the negative, or maintain a successful level of performance. The Goals divide the Mission into its most critical parts.

- Improve/increase/raise/expand (performance numbers go up)
- Reduce/decrease/lower/prevent/avoid (performance numbers go down)
- Develop/achieve/initiate/open/start new (new performance numbers)
- Maintain/continue/sustain (performance numbers remain the same)

Example of a Good Goal (in bold italic):

Organization Mission: Reduce diabetes in our community.

> **Good Goal:** ***Reduce new incidents of diabetes*** by expanding education programs. (Manager Title)
>
> **Analysis:** The Mission is to reduce diabetes. The Goal is to "reduce new cases" of diabetes by expanding educational programs. If diabetic cases continue to grow, then obviously the education program may not be working. Whereas, if diabetic cases begin to decrease where the education program was given, then the case could be made that the organization is successfully meeting its Mission to reduce diabetes by achieving its Goal. Having data showing success could result in obtaining more funding. Funding sources like to fund successful programs.

Example of a Poor Goal (in bold italic):

Organization Mission: Reduce diabetes in our community.

Poor Goal: *Educate the public* about the risks of diabetes. (Manager Title)

Analysis: The Goal to "educate" is a Function. This can lead to measuring success by the number of pamphlets, presentations, and public service announcements. Though the incidences of diabetes might go up, the Goal could be seen as successful because it was to "educate." Meanwhile, the Mission to reduce diabetes could be failing. Education could be an Objective or Strategy in support of reducing diabetes but would still require a measurement showing if education was decreasing diabetes.

More Examples of Goals (in bold italic):

Telecommunications Company's Mission: Improve cell phone customers' experience by delivering exceptional services and products at affordable prices.

Goals:

- *Improve* customer experience. (Manager Title)
- *Expand* service availability. (Manager Title)
- *Reduce* customer costs. (Manager Title)

Analysis: Each Goal focuses on a major part of the company. The first Goal of improving customers' experience is the most important Goal. The second Goal deals with better availability to the customer. The third Goal is to reduce customer costs.

Packing/Shipping Company's Mission: Deliver customer packages on time, undamaged, and at an affordable rate.

Goals:

- *Reduce package shipment times.* (Manager Title)
- *Reduce damage* to customer products by improving handling processes. (Manager Title)
- *Reduce costs* by improving shipping efficiencies. (Manager Title)

Analysis: The Mission could describe just about any shipping company and that's a good thing. Remember, organizations of a similar nature usually have similar Mission and Goals. These Goals focus on the prime activities that affect customers.

Sole Proprietor Shoe Repair Store's Mission: Repair a shoe that stays repaired.

Goals:

- **Repair customers' shoes to as new of a condition** as possible.
- **Shine the customer's shoes to the brightest shine** using quality products.
- **Help the customer maintain the shoe in good condition** through education.

Analysis: This example appears to be over simplified but in fact, a small company's Mission and Goals are at ground level. The owner looks into a mirror and asks, "What level of service do my customers want?" "If I was having my shoes repaired, what kind of service would I like to receive?" If the business expands (e.g., selling shoes and socks), then the Mission will need to be modified and new Goals added.

Small Restaurant's Mission: Provide delicious, affordable, and nutritious meals in a clean and inviting environment.

Goals:

- **Improve customers' menu selection** by adding delicious and nutritious meals. (Manager Title)
- **Maintain affordable meals** by managing costs. (Manager Title)
- **Improve customers' experience** by creating a warm and inviting environment by treating customers with respect and by keeping the restaurant exceptionally clean. (Manager Title)

Analysis: In this example, management wants to improve the overall performance of the restaurant by providing good food, clean environment, affordable, and a cherished experience. The key activity words become the Goals. Once these Goals are achieved, then the Goals can be changed to "maintain" or "continue to provide." The second Goal demonstrates a Goal that maintains an activity.

Charity Organization's Mission: *Improve lives of young people* by mobilizing the caring power of communities to advance the common good.

Goals:

- *Improve* student's success in life by improving educational programs. (Manager Title)
- Help students *achieve* financial stability by promoting job training and placement. (Manager Title)
- *Reduce* cases of malnutrition through improved nutritional programs. (Manager Title)

Analysis: The Goals contain a strong and focused customer end-result. The keywords of "improve, achieve, and reduce" can measure success. Each Goal contains the "how" aspect of attaining the Mission.

Diabetes Group's Mission: Improve the lives of people by preventing and managing diabetes.

Goals:

- *Improve diabetics' lives* by instituting proven diabetes management techniques. (Manager Title)
- *Reduce diabetes* through educational programs. (Manager Title)
- *Reduce diabetes* through the early detection of diabetes. (Manager Title)

Analysis: The Mission is strong, "prevent and manage diabetes." The three Goals cite significant activities: improve diabetics' lives and reduce diabetes through education and detection. These Goals represent the measurements for success.

National Association's Mission: Ensure the political, educational, social, and economic equality of rights for all persons.

Goals:

- *Improve* the equality of rights and reduce race prejudice. (Manager Title)
- *Remove* all racial discrimination through democratic processes. (Manager Title)
- *Secure the civil rights* through the enactment and enforcement of Federal, state, and local laws. (Manager Title)
- *Reduce racial discrimination* by educating the public of the adverse effects of racial discrimination. (Manager Title)
- *Ensure people receive equal treatment* under the law and the constitution when exercising their rights. (Manager Title)

Analysis: Each Goal has a measured action: improve, remove, secure, reduce, and ensure. Some Goals appear to be overlapping but should be distinguishable when taking into account the different Objectives that would support each Goal.

Environmental Agency's Mission: Protect human health and the environment.

Goals:

- *Improve* air quality. (Manager Title)

- *Improve* community efforts to return to a clean environment. (Manager Title)

- *Advance* sustainable growth through educational programs. (Manager Title)

- *Protect* the environment by ensuring the safe handling of chemicals. (Manager Title)

- *Improve* the environment through improved pollution monitoring. (Manager Title)

- Help industries *reduce* pollution through improved pollution control devices. (Manager Title)

Analysis: The Goals use strongly worded action verbs that can be measured for success, such as improve, protect, reduce, and advance. These are long-term Goals work to improve a certain performance level. Because they are agency-level Goals, the targeted levels of performance are generalized. Specific numbers would be stated in the Objectives or Strategies that support the Goals or in a separate "Performance Measurements" section of the plan.

City Police Department's Mission: Protect citizens from crime, to be secure in their possessions, and to live in peace.

Goals:

- *Reduce* crime. (Manager Title)
- *Apprehend* offenders. (Manager Title)
- *Improve recovery and return* of stolen property. (Manager Title)
- *Improve* traffic through enforcement. (Manager Title)
- *Improve* law enforcement effectiveness through interdepartmental cooperation. (Manager Title)

Analysis: All the Goals can be measured using crime statistics that will indicate the impact to the community. Ultimately, a safe, prosperous, and productive community may also be measurements for success.

Public Agency's Mission: Improve the physical, mental, emotional, and environmental health of the community.

Goals:

- *Help children grow up happy, healthy, confident, and secure.* (Manager Title)
- *Provide a safe and healthy air, water, and food environment* where people live, work, and play. (Manager Title)
- *Prevent and prepare against threats to health and safety* through coordinated efforts across the country. (Manager Title)
- *Improve personal and collective health and well-being* by providing support and information needed to make healthy choices. (Manager Title)

Analysis: This agency has four Missions: physical, mental, emotional, and environmental. The Goals are specific. What activities would support the Goals? Which part of the Mission is supported by which Goal(s)?

Examples of Actual Federal Agency Goals: The following examples demonstrate strong, decisive Goals that provide a strong indicator of success.

- **Federal Emergency Management Agency:** Improve delivery of aid to disaster victims.
- **General Services Administration:** Find the right agency on the first try.
- **Immigration and Naturalization Service:** Reduce clearance time at U.S. airports.
- **Occupational Safety and Health Administration:** Reduce injury and illnesses in the workplace.
- **National Park Service:** Expand access to Federal recreation opportunities.
- **Social Security Administration:** Improve access to Social Security information.

Lower-level and Internal Goals: Goals for the lower-level components within an organization focus on improving or managing internal processes, manufacturing, administrative functions, business activities, etc., that support the higher-level Goals. Lower-level Goals can be accomplished within a shorter time period (within a year or two).

Examples of lower-level Goals:

- Reduce defective parts by 50% within next 11 months. Requirements: 4 staff and $14K. (Manager Title)

- Develop a process within the next three months to deliver products within one hour upon receipt of order. Requirements: 1 staff and $3.5K. (Manager Title)

- Improve sales by 11 percent within the next 22 months using new marketing techniques. Requirements: 6 staff and $20K. (Manager Title)

- Reduce production time from 3 hours to 2 hours within next 7 months. Requirements: 23 staff and $150K. (Manager Title)

- Reduce patient's waiting time to within 10 minutes. Requirements: 3 nurses (1 per shift) and $120K per year. (Manager Title)

These lower-level targets should have some basis. Spend the time to identify the resources and the time needed to achieve the targets. Also, if your organization has a good planning methodology at lower organizational levels, continue using it and just refer to it in the organization's Strategic Plan. If it becomes evident that the time and resource estimates were off, adjust the higher Goals' required resources to reflect the new reality.

SUMMARY: Goals should be the most significant and important end-result activities to be accomplished by the organization for the customer. All activities within the organization should support one or more Goals. Any activity that does not support a Goal should either be stopped or a Goal should be added that would include the activity, or amend a current Goal to cover the lower activity.

I strongly recommend that the responsible manager's title for each Goal be cited so that the organization will know who is responsible for that Goal. This will help managers stay focused on their assigned Goal(s).

D. Objective

> A short-term but major activity for accomplishing a Goal.

An Objective is where the rubber meets the road. An Objective can be described as:

- A major initiative(s) needed to be achieved in the organization's effort to accomplish a Goal. Answers the question, what action must be taken to achieve the Goal. It is a major but specific and clearly defined activity or task.

- Having significant and defined resources and effort (funding, staffing, resources, technology, expertise, actions, etc.)

- Having a significant impact on the organization's product.

- Activities which the organization has control or influence.

- Being achieved in chronological order with or independent from other Objectives.

- An activity that can be measured as to whether the Objective is being achieved or not.

- Influential on a Goal's Performance Measurement.

- Having a real targeted completion date based upon analysis, not on an arbitrary date.

- A contract between the management in charge of accomplishing the Objective and the management in charge of the Goal it supports.

Objectives might address the following activities:

- Product performance
- Financial issues
- Production
- Product development
- Quality control
- Operations/Processes/Manufacturing
- Internal administrative improvements
- Marketing
- Technology
- Education/training
- Timeliness
- Sales
- Administrative

The above activities are generic and how they are written depends on the wording of the Goal that they support. An Objective that states, "improve product reliability" may support a Goal to deliver the best turn-key computer system or maintain customer's productivity.

Also, an Objective to "Improve response time to customer inquires . . ." may be one of several Objectives to address customer service inquires. Another Objective may contain the same beginning, "improve response time . . ." but ends with, "by expanding training program for call center employees" or "by increasing customer service staff."

In some cases, the Objective may simply say, "Improve response time to customer inquires," and the Strategies may address the more specific solutions for improving training or increasing staffing. What is important is that the Objective clearly supports a Goal by accomplishing a more detailed and specific action.

General Examples of Objectives:

- Increase annual sales
- Improve product reliability
- Reduce overhead costs
- Improve response time to customer inquires by implementing electronic texting capabilities
- Improve response time to customer inquires by expanding the call centers
- Improve delivery times by developing new shipping procedures
- Increase client base by expanding marketing and branding approaches
- Expand customer choices by developing new and improved products
- Expand customer choices with new and improved products by raising investment capital
- Improve manufacturing performance for product quality, customer service, timeliness, etc.
- Expand sales training
- Upgrade technology
- Expand service area
- Increase marketing
- Expand customer base by implementing cloud and virtual technology

- Reduce diabetes through education
- Reduce diabetes through research
- Reduce diabetes by increasing screenings

Resource Requirements: The resource numbers come from the list of required resources from the supporting Strategies (which will be covered after this discussion concerning Objectives).

Sometimes the Objective numbers (staff, cost, and schedule) may not match with the total of the Strategies' numbers if some staff members or resources support more than one Strategy. What is important is that a resource analysis has been conducted so that management has an idea of the resources needed for achieving or working towards the Objective. The analysis also influences the decision as to whether or not to go on with the planned Objective.

The analysis won't be easy. No more pie-in-sky estimates but a real analysis. It will require real thinking to figure out what must be done and how it can be done. Having the manager's title connected to the Objective also provides a real incentive to accomplish the Objective.

The following examples demonstrate this process in which the Objective supports a Goal. Examples include businesses, non-profits, and government agencies.

BIG BUSINESS EXAMPLES:

Telecommunications Company Mission: Improve customers' cell phone experience by delivering exceptional services and products at affordable prices.

Goal: Expand service availability. (Manager Title)

Objective: Add two new customer call centers. Requirements: Staff-82, Cost-$850K, Schedule-fourteen months. (Manager Title)

Goal: Reduce customer costs. (Manager Title)

Objective: Develop affordable short-term contracts. Requirements: Staff-3, Cost-$150K, Schedule-eight months. (Manager Title)

Analysis: The above business Objectives cite specific actions that will be conducted within a defined time frame. The staff, cost, and schedule numbers come from a total of the resources identified at the Strategy level. These requirements should be based upon a true analysis of the effort needed to accomplish the Objective. You might be able to cite a targeted measurement (e.g., reduced customer costs by 5%), based upon your analysis.

Each Objective supports the same long-term Performance Measurement of improving customer experience. Adding call centers or lower cost contracts will certainly improve customer experience. The Objectives may continue until they have reached the point of diminished return. That is, adding more centers or providing short-term contacts will no longer increase customers' experience. At that point, the Objectives need to be evaluated and possibly replaced with something new.

Packing/Shipping Company's Mission: Deliver customer packages on time, undamaged, and at an affordable rate.

Goals: Reduce damage to customer products by improving the handling processes. (Manager Title)

Objective: Improve packaging techniques.

Requirements: Cost-$15K, Schedule-two months. (Manager Title)

Objective: Instruct packers on safe handling procedures
Requirements: Cost-$11K, Schedule-four weeks. (Manager Title)

Analysis: The Objectives are specific enough for the company to initiate. The Objectives can be conducted independent of each other.

SMALL BUSINESS EXAMPLE:

Shoe Repair Mission: Repair a shoe that stays repaired.

Goal: Repair customers' shoes to as new a condition as possible.

Objective: Upgrade stitching equipment.
Requirements: Cost-$1.9K, Schedule-two months.

Objective: Improve repair of synthetic materials by receiving training.
Requirements: Cost-$500, Schedule-three day course.

Analysis: The Objectives are specific. In fact, the owner could skip Objectives and simply list these actions as Strategies. I've skipped inserting the Manager's Title because the business is too small to require it.

Small Restaurant's Mission: Provide delicious, affordable, and nutritious meals in a clean and inviting environment.

Goals: Maintain affordable meals by managing costs.

Objective: Negotiate lower bulk purchasing rates to lower unit costs.
Requirements: Cost-no cost, Schedule-Ongoing activity.

Objective: Reduce costs by cooking smaller portions to reduce end-of-day waste.
Requirements: Cost-no cost, Schedule-Ongoing activity.

Analysis: In these cases, the Objectives are not cost activities but rather a human activity to identify and negotiate for a lower bulk price and to reduce waste by improving cooking schedules so there is less waste at the end of the day. I've skipped putting in the "Manager Title" because the owner will know exactly who is responsible for what.

NON-PROFIT EXAMPLE:

Charity Organization's Mission: Improve lives of young people by mobilizing the caring power of communities to advance the common good.

Goals: Help students achieve financial stability by promoting job training and placement. (Manager Title)

Objective: Create training classes for skills that have a high probability of success for the students in the future.
Requirements: Staff-five, Cost-$20K, Schedule-seven months. (Manager Title)

Objective: Expand job training classes by obtaining local, state, and Federal grants.
Requirements: Staff-one, Cost-$3K, Schedule-Ongoing activity. (Manager Title)

Analysis: Each Objective is a major activity to help create job training that will assist in the students' future success.

Diabetes Group's Mission: Improve the lives of people by preventing and managing diabetes.

Goal: Reduce diabetes through educational programs. (Director of Public Affairs)

Objective: Initiate diabetes educational programs at the elementary and high schools.
Requirements: Staff-three, Cost-$15K, Schedule-six months. (Manager Title)

Objective: Provide diabetes educational programs to the medical community.
Requirements: Staff-two, Cost-$45K, Schedule-eighteen months. (Manager Title)

Goal: Reduce diabetes through the early detection of diabetes. (Director of Medical Programs)

Objective: Expand accessibility for free diabetes testing by civic organizations.
Requirements: Staff-three, Cost-$11K, Schedule-ten months. (Manager Title)

Objective: Increase local health facilities' diabetic screening programs.
Requirements: Staff-two, Cost-$9K, Schedule-eight months. (Manager Title)

Analysis: The Mission has two Goals for reducing diabetes: education and early detection. The Objectives describe activities needed for achieving the Goals. There would probably be additional Goals to address the Mission of managing diabetes.

The first Goal would cost $60K with Objectives needing six and eighteen months. The Second Goal requires $20K with the Objectives needing ten and eight months. A flow chart (Gantt chart) within the Strategic Planning document could clarify the schedule for these Goals and Objectives.

The overall Performance Measurement for the Goals and Objectives would be a reduction of diabetes in the community. Each Objective would have a corresponding Measurement. For example:

Goal: Reduce diabetes through educational programs.

Objective: Initiate diabetes educational programs at the elementary and high schools.

Short-Term, Output Measurement: Number of schools conducting educational programs to reduce diabetes.

Long-Term, Outcome Result Measurement: Reduction in the number of diabetic cases in the schools.

GOVERNMENT EXAMPLE:

Environmental Agency's Mission: Protect human health and the environment.

Goals: Improve Air Quality. (Manager Title)

Objective: Achieve and maintain health-based air pollution standards and reduce risk from toxic air pollutants and indoor air contaminants.
Requirements: Staff-2,000, Cost-$250m, Schedule-12 years. (Manager Title)

Objective: Protect the public from the harmful effects of ultraviolet radiation by restoring the earth's stratospheric ozone layer.
Requirements: Staff-350, Cost-$100m, Schedule-8 years. (Manager Title)

Objective: Protect the public from unnecessary releases of radiation and to minimize impacts should unwanted releases occur.
Requirements: Staff-285, Cost-$300m, Schedule-3 years. (Manager Title)

Analysis: The Goals and Objectives are broad actions. Staff, cost, and schedules are large. More specific actions will be described at the plan's Strategy/Tactical level. (Note: The numbers for the requirements are made up. The real numbers would most likely be much higher.)

City Police Department's Mission: Protect citizens from crime, to be secure in their possessions, and to live in peace.

Goals: Improve the recovery and return of stolen property. (Manager Title)

Objective: Improve the rate of returned stolen property to the rightful owners by automating the process to cross-check lost articles against found articles.
Requirements: Staff-one plus contractor, Cost-$125K, Schedule-eight months. (Manager Title)

Objective: Develop the ability to photograph recovered items for identification purposes.
Requirements: Staff-two, Cost-$25K, Schedule-one month. (Manager Title)

Analysis: The Objectives will improve the ability to return stolen property to its owner (customer). The first Objective will require a contractor to develop the automated process. The specific contract resources may or may not be available or appropriate to disclose until after the contract award, at which time, the cost and effort can be added to the plan.

SUMMARY: Look at your Goal Statements and ask, "What major activities must my organization conduct to accomplish each Goal?" A successful organization is going to go through this process so why not make it part of your plan? Once the required resources have been determined under the Strategy section, you can evaluate the total resources required for each Objective.

E. Strategy

> **A concrete and specific action for accomplishing an Objective.**

We've gone from Mission to Goal to Objective. We are now in the trenches of the organization where we have Strategy - an action or list of actions that need to be started and accomplished if the Objective is to be achieved. This is where your organization is today. Look down at your feet. You are about to take one or more steps to move from where you are today to where you need to be tomorrow. These immediate actions would be identified during the planning process and connect to your Strategic Plan as key Strategies to be accomplished. All these little Strategies accomplished today and tomorrow will eventually accomplish the plan's Goals and Objectives in the future.

A Strategy can be described as:

- A specific, visible action or series of actions that must be completed in order to accomplish the Objective.//
- Having a defined beginning and end.
- Being achieved in chronological order with or independent from other Strategies.
- Activities which the organization has control or influence.
- A contract with the management in charge of the Objective.
- An activity where the resources, funding, technology, expertise, personnel, etc., have been identified, are available, and/or committed.

Strategies are identified after a careful analysis of the:

- Actions needed to accomplish an Objective.
- Required and available resources.
- Customer and stakeholder requirements.
- Risks.
- PRMs.
- Business and market atmosphere.
- Any other analysis that will identify and initiate a good Strategy.

Now, the fine strategic details for each component within the organization would not be listed under the organization's Strategic Plan's Strategies but in a separate Tactical Plan, Plan of Action, Action Plan, Business Plan, Program Plan, or whatever you want to call it. Missing this connection between the Strategic Plan and a Tactical Plan is another reason why Strategic Plans are less than successful. The Strategic Plan may be ignored over time as an organization conducts activities that do not follow or support the Strategic Plan.

Once the organization's Mission, Goals, and Objectives have been defined, the key managers must conduct an educated and "best-guess" analysis on what activities need to be accomplished to achieve the Objectives. The Strategies are then presented to the next upper-level management for approval.

A good analysis will disclose any weak or overly optimistic Objectives and will require management to revisit and evaluate the Objectives. The Strategy offers a check and balance approach. The entire initial Strategic Planning process is a give and take process where senior management identifies the big picture but it's the lower-level management that must craft the Strategies for accomplishing the plan. General Eisenhower may have selected the major Goals for Allied forces in World War II, but it was the military units on the ground, air, and sea whose Strategies eventually achieved the General's Goals and Objectives.

NOTE: Part VII, *Analysis*, will describe ways to develop the Strategies and action items that eventually become the planning Strategies.

Let's see how this works. We'll work our way down from the Mission Statement through the Goal to the Objective, and to the Strategy. The Strategies are just samples and do not include every action needed to support the Objective. I have not listed specific resource requirements for the Strategies because it would serve no purpose for these examples.

BIG BUSINESS EXAMPLE:

Telecommunications Company Mission: Improve customers' cell phone experience by delivering exceptional services and products at affordable prices.

Goal: Expand service availability. (Manager Title) (Resource Requirements)

Objective: Add two new customer call centers.
Requirements: Staff-82, Cost-$850K, Schedule-fourteen months. (Manager Title)

> **Strategy:** Locate the best locations for call centers. (Manager Title) (Resource Requirements)
>
> **Strategy:** Conduct design and construction activities. (Manager Title) (Resource Requirements)
>
> **Strategy:** Set up training schedule for new employees (Manager Title) (Resource Requirements)
>
> **Strategy:** Identify procurement schedule for all physical components, such as furniture, technology, inventory items, etc. (Manager Title) (Resource Requirements)

Analysis: The list of Strategies provide examples of the activities for expanding the customer base with two new call centers. I've not included resource requirements but there certainly will be estimates as the business gathers information on the effort, cost, and schedule for each Strategy. Each Strategy will require its own Tactical Plan which contains the specific activities needed to support the Strategy.

Packing/Shipping Company's Mission: Deliver customer packages on time, undamaged, and at an affordable rate.

> **Goals:** Reduce damage to customer products by improving the handling processes. (Manager Title)
>
> > **Objective:** Improve packaging techniques.
> > Requirements: Cost-$15K, Schedule-two months. (Manager Title)

Strategy: Research packing techniques with a proven record of protecting products. (Manager Title) (Resource Requirements)

Strategy: Based on research, procure packaging that provides improved protection to packed items. (Manager Title) (Resource Requirements)

Objective: Instruct packers on safe handling procedures. Requirements: Cost-$11K, Schedule-four weeks. (Manager Title)

Strategy: Contract professional instructors with experience in packaging (Manager Title) (Resource Requirements)

Strategy: Set up training schedules. (Manager Title) (Resource Requirements)

Analysis: The Strategies are fairly basic and may be the responsibility of the Objective's manager.

SMALL BUSINESS EXAMPLE:

Shoe Repair Mission: Repair a shoe that stays repaired.

Goal: Repair customers' shoes to as new a condition as possible.

Objective: Upgrade stitching equipment.
Requirements: Cost-$1.9K, Schedule-two months.

Strategy: Identify upgraded stitching equipment.

Strategy: Ensure adequate space and power available for new equipment.

Strategy: Order upgraded stitching equipment.

Strategy: Install new stitching equipment.

Strategy: Sell old equipment.

Objective: Improve the repairing of synthetic materials by receiving training.
Requirements: Cost-$500, Schedule-three day course.

> **Strategy:** Arrange for part-time help to manage store during training.
>
> **Strategy:** Submit registration and tuition.
>
> **Strategy:** Schedule travel and lodging for training class.
>
> **Strategy:** Attend training.
>
> **Strategy:** Initiate improved shoe repair techniques.

Analysis: Because the Objectives are specific, the Strategies are detailed. Strategies can be a specific list of actions to be performed.

Small Restaurant's Mission: Provide delicious, affordable, and nutritious meals in a clean and inviting environment.

> **Goals:** Maintain affordable meals by managing costs. (Manager Title)
>
> **Objective:** Negotiate bulk purchasing rates to lower unit costs.
> Requirements: Cost-no cost, Schedule-Ongoing activity.
>
>> **Strategy:** Arrange meetings with suppliers.
>>
>> **Strategy:** Prepare negotiation strategy to get prices lowered.
>>
>> **Strategy:** Negotiate lower prices with suppliers.
>
> **Objective:** Reduce costs by cooking smaller portions to reduce end-of-day waste.
> Requirements: Cost-no cost, Schedule-Ongoing activity.
>
>> **Strategy:** Identify foods that are most wasted at the end of the day.

Strategy: Set up cooking schedule to reduce cooking of foods wasted at the end of the day.

Strategy: Reduce food proportions wasted by customers.

Analysis: As with the shoe repair business, the Strategies are specific. A small business would most likely have a list of activities that need to be continually conducted in support of an Objective.

NON-PROFIT EXAMPLE:

Charity Organization's Mission: Improve lives of young people by mobilizing the caring power of communities to advance the common good.

Goals: Help students achieve financial stability by promoting job training and placement. (Manager Title)

Objective: Create training classes for skills that have a high probability of success for the students in the future. Requirements: Staff-five, Cost-$20K, Schedule-seven months. (Manager Title)

Strategy: Identify the skills that society will require in the future.

Strategy: Hire instructors.

Strategy: Identify and procure adequate classroom and supplies.

Strategy: Schedule classes.

Strategy: Conduct classes.

Objective: Expand job training classes by obtaining local, state, and Federal grants.

Requirements: Staff-one, Cost-$3K, Schedule-Ongoing activity. (Manager Title)

Strategy: Contract a grant writer.

Strategy: Identify grants relevant to training.

Strategy: Apply for grants.

Analysis: Non-Profit organizations are no different from other organizations. With the right Mission Statement, the key Goals, Objectives, and Strategies can be easily identified and initiated.

Diabetes Group's Mission: Improve the lives of people by preventing and managing diabetes.

Goal: Reduce diabetes through educational programs. (Director of Public Affairs)

Objective: Initiate diabetes educational programs at the elementary and high schools.
Requirements: Staff-three, Cost-$15K, Schedule-six months. (Manager Title)

Strategy: Establish liaison with elementary and high schools.

Strategy: Develop educational programs geared for school children.

Strategy: Train staff to effectively present programs.

Strategy: Initiate training programs.

Objective: Provide diabetes educational programs to the medical community.
Requirements: Staff-two, Cost-$45K, Schedule-eighteen months. (Manager Title)

Strategy: Develop educational programs geared to the medical community.

Strategy: Contact all local medical facilities and offer educational programs.

Strategy: Establish a schedule for programs over the next twelve months.

Strategy: Start programs.

Goal: Reduce diabetes through the early detection of diabetes. (Director of Medical Programs)

Objective: Expand accessibility for free diabetes testing by civic organizations.
Requirements: Staff-three, Cost-$11K, Schedule-ten months. (Manager Title)

Strategy: Identify funding for free diabetes testing.

Strategy: Recruit civic organizations to conduct testing.

Strategy: Hire trained staff to test for diabetes.

Strategy: Purchase diabetes testing equipment and supplies.

Strategy: Begin diabetes testing.

Objective: Increase local health facilities' diabetic screening programs.
Requirements: Staff-two, Cost-$9K, Schedule-eight months. (Manager Title)

Strategy: Develop a persuasive presentation on the importance for diabetic screening.

Strategy: Train staff to give presentation.

Strategy: Establish liaison with local health facilities.

Strategy: Initiate screening programs.

Analysis: You can see how the trickle down affect occurs as the planning effort drills down to an organization's lower level. There is a definite connection from the Mission to the Strategy. It would be of value to insert the manager's title if each Strategy has a different manager.

The overall Performance Measurement for confirming the Mission and its Goals would be the reduction of diabetes in the community. Once the Strategies have been accomplished (short-term measurements), then the Objective's long-term measurements can be gathered. Here is an example:

Mission: *Prevent and cure diabetes.*

Goal: Reduce diabetes through educational programs.

> **Objective:** Initiate diabetes educational programs at the elementary and high schools.
>
> > **Short-Term, Output Measurement:** Number of programs completed.
> >
> > **Long-Term, Outcome Results Measurements:**
> >
> > 1) Reduction in obese children
> >
> > 2) Improved health of diabetics
> >
> > 3) Reduction in children becoming diabetic

GOVERNMENT EXAMPLE:

Environmental Agency's Mission: Protect human health and the environment.

> **Goals:** Improve Air Quality. (Manager Title)

Objective: Achieve and maintain health-based air pollution standards and reduce risk from toxic air pollutants and indoor air contaminants.
Requirements: Staff-2,000, Cost-$250m, Schedule-12 years. (Manager Title)

> **Strategy:** Identify health-based air pollution standards. (Manager Title) (Resource Requirements)
>
> **Strategy:** Identify and chart the potential costs to accomplish each Strategy. (Manager Title) (Resource Requirements)
>
> **Strategy:** Initiate programs to meet air pollution standards. (Manager Title) (Resource Requirements)

Objective: Protect the public from the harmful effects of ultraviolet radiation by restoring the earth's stratospheric ozone layer.
Requirements: Staff-350, Cost-$100m, Schedule-8 years. (Manager Title)

> **Strategy:** Create standards and regulations to minimize ozone damage. (Manager Title) (Resource Requirements)
>
> **Strategy:** Identify solutions to minimize the release of ozone damaging chemicals and gases. (Manager Title) (Resource Requirements)

Objective: Protect the public from unnecessary releases of radiation and to minimize impacts should unwanted releases occur.
Requirements: Staff-285, Cost-$300m, Schedule-3 years. (Manager Title)

> **Strategy:** Identify solutions to minimize the release of radiation. (Manager Title) (Resource Requirements)

Strategy: Implement disaster plans to reduce impact of significant radiation emissions. (Manager Title) (Resource Requirements)

Analysis: With large organizations, the Objectives and Strategies must be general and broad. Note that the Strategies are separate activities from each other. Large organizations' Strategies are usually not conducted in chronological order but are separate major activities.

City Police Department's Mission: Protect citizens from crime, to be secure in their possessions, and to live in peace.

Goals: Improve the recovery and return of stolen property. (Manager Title)

Objective: Improve the rate of returned stolen property to the rightful owners by automating the process to cross-check lost articles against found articles.
Requirements: Staff-one plus contractor, Cost-$125K, Schedule-eight months. (Manager Title)

Strategy: Identify requirements and cost estimates.

Strategy: Acquire funding.

Strategy: Contract for technology.

Strategy: Expand facility to accommodate new system.

Strategy: Build the system

Strategy: Train employees

Strategy: Implement the system

Objective: Develop the ability to photograph recovered items for identification purposes.

Requirements: Staff-two, Cost-$25K, Schedule-one month. (Manager Title)

    Strategy: Identify requirements and cost estimates.

    Strategy: Acquire funding.

    Strategy: Contract for technology.

    Strategy: Implement photo program.

Analysis: There will be an extensive and detailed list of Strategies needed to be conducted in order to accomplish the Objectives. These Strategies are only generalized samples.

As you can see above, as you drill down through the plan, actions to be taken become more specific. How specific they become depends on where you are in the organization. For example, the environmental agency's Strategies are broad. The specific components will need to develop more specific Tactical Plans to outline the actual activities, schedules, and costs needed for accomplishing or striving to accomplish the agency-level Objectives.

Whereas, a small organization may only need one overall plan in which the Strategies will list specific actions to be taken. Certainly the day-to-day details are not included but the small organization will manage those details on a daily basis.

As with Objectives, it's critical that the Strategies list the required resources to validate that a resource analysis has been conducted. The resource list might need adjustment as Strategies change to accomplish the Objective. For large organizations, the Strategies would also list the responsible manager.

NOTE: In some cases, Objective and Strategy statements may or may not contain measurements regarding activity, schedule, and cost. At the early stages of planning, it might not be possible to say that an Objective will be accomplished in xx months or something will improve by xx percentage. As the organization moves forward, there should be activity, schedule, and cost charts produced and attached to each Objective and Strategy that documents the best-guess estimates regarding the required effort.

SUMMARY: What has been described at this point is a Strategic Planning format for the top of the organization. A large organization starts with an executive-level Strategic Plan in which its branches, divisions, and sections have secondary Strategic Plans that support the overall plan.

A "one-size-fits all" Strategic Planning approach does not work at all levels of the organization. As one moves down into the organization, the plans become narrow, specific, and detailed. When developing a plan at an organization's lower areas, the plan may need to eliminate the Objective category rather than squeezing it in between Goals and Strategies.

For example, a small call center unit of 20 employees has the Function to answer initial support calls. The unit has the one Goal to direct incoming calls to the correct support service the first time. Rather than creating an Objective, skip the Objective and going straight into Strategies to provide specific actions to be taken - hire people skilled in dealing with customers and conduct ongoing staff training on directing calls correctly the first time. In this example, Strategies support a Goal.

F. PRMs (Performance and Results Measurements)

> The results to be achieved for the customer.

PRMs answer the question, is the organization achieving its Mission? Has your product's reliability met the customers' expectations? Has the organization's actions reduced diabetes? Has your software solution helped the customers succeed? Is the government achieving its mandated, legislative solution?

All organizations measure Function Performance (e.g., how many widgets sold, how many customers served, how many applications processed). These are all good measurements. A successful organization, however, needs to measure its customers' success in using or receiving the organization's products. Is the customer satisfied? Have you provided what the customer needs, wants, or expects?

PRMs also provide an early warning of a potential problem or failure. The sooner an organization identifies and corrects a problem, the more likely it will avoid failure. And it's not just a matter of collecting data. It's about reading, understanding, and interpreting what the data measurement tells you. If targeted PRMs are not being achieved, an organization can develop and implement changes to bring performance back in line for achieving the Mission and providing the results expected by the customer.

PRMs should be feasible, but not the path of least resistance. They usually are the most difficult measurements to obtain. Good Performance Goals and Objectives are based on the outcomes and results to the customer. A popular saying among strategists is, "What gets measured gets done."

An organization needs to identify PRMs when building the Strategic Plan. Thereafter, new measurements can be added as needed. Unexpected changes in customer requirements, technology, legislation, market direction, etc., can trigger the need for updated or new PRMs.

What type of PRMs to use depends on where you are in the organization. The top of the organization measures positive and negative outcomes (e.g., number of satisfied or dissatisfied customers, decrease or increase of a disease, improvement or deterioration of social issues). Internal organizational components have operational measurements (e.g., sales figures, products returned, response times, repeat customers) which eventually reflect customer satisfaction. Staff members may also have their own individual PRMs which support broader performance measures.

PRMs go hand in hand with the Mission. It can be said that:

- A Mission requires PRMs.
- PRMs require a Mission.

PRMs can be described by the following statements:

- Customer's success with the organization's product
- Mission status
- Positive or negative affect on the customer
- Results which the organization can change or influence
- Difficult to obtain
- Reflect program's effectiveness
- How projects and activities are working in practice
- Standards or baselines to be met or exceeded

- Disclose problems
- Identify processes to be improved
- Measure accomplishments
- Reveal an effort's effectiveness

Organizations often fail to perform PRMs because they:

- Lack viable and active Strategic Planning processes within the organization.
- Fail to embrace performance management.
- Lack commitment, sufficient funding, and/or technical competency to successfully collect and analyze data on an ongoing basis.
- Cannot sustain the performance management process in the face of budget cuts and scarce or reduced resources.
- Lack customer or stakeholder input.
- Have incomplete requirements and specifications.
- Lack executive support.
- Have unrealistic timeframes.
- Have too many measures, rather than selecting key measurements.
- Have no understanding or appreciation of PRMs' value.
- Only want easy Function measurements which appear relevant without really indicating results.
- Have incorrect Mission and Goals that are focused on Functions.

Types of Measurements: Throughout our lifetime, we measure things that we buy, use, build, and do. Most measurements are basic arithmetic; some are "best guesses" while others are complex formulas. We measure things on a frequent basis to ensure that we do something correctly. We also measure to successfully achieve the future. Let's look at how organizations measure by Function and Performance.

Function (Output): Output measures the most common and easiest activities conducted by the organization, such as:

- Human and capital resources applied and invested to produce the product.

    Example: Funding, staffing, production costs, procurement, unit cost, administrative and overhead costs, training, marketing, advertising, etc.

- Internal efficiencies.

    Example: The time, effort, and cost it takes to manufacture a product.

- Activities relating to the product.

    Example: Measures sales, customers served, market share, product production numbers, service calls, warranty work, etc.

Performance (Outcome/Result): Outcome measures the customer's success, such as:

- The organization's value to its customer. The expected, desired, or actual result the product has on the intended customer. Said another way, did the customers get what they wanted or needed?

    Example: Did the customer's car drive 200,000 miles without one single mechanical breakdown? Did the computer software complete the required tasks? Did that accountant find all the possible tax exemptions available to you? Did the repaired shoe stay repaired? Was that the best carrot cake you ever ate?

- The customer accomplishments or satisfaction as a result of the organization's efforts to accomplish its Mission.

  Example: Has the medical clinic's newer equipment cured or successfully treated more patients? Are there fewer HIV cases as a result of medical intervention? Does that new winter jacket keep you warmer?

- Deeper or indirect consequences resulting from achieving program Goals.

  Example: With a cleaner environment, has productivity increased or have people had fewer environmentally-related illnesses? Do automobile drivers experience fewer accidents as a result of new safety devices on automobiles, etc.?

Generally, an organization will first identify the current level of customer or product performance - customer satisfaction, number of repeat customers, number of products returned, growth of a social or medical problem, demand for innovative technology, etc. Once a baseline is established and after careful analysis, an organization can target a specific and achievable performance number that would define success - increase satisfied customers by 26% or decrease customer's dissatisfaction by 26% (two different ways to measure the same outcome), or if carbon pollution is reduced by 15%, the incidents of a particular disease should be reduced by 25%.

Measurements are described as numbers in an objective and statistical point of view. Are sales going up or down? Are satisfied customers increasing or decreasing? Some measurements may look at the customer qualitatively by asking how does the customer feel about the product? Eventually, however, qualitative, survey-type data will be expressed in numbers.

EXAMPLES OF MEASUREMENTS:

U.S. Coast Guard (source: USCG web site - 2011)

Safety:

Output Measures (Functions):

- Conducted more than 70,000 commercial inspections of U.S. flagged vessels
- Performed more than 12,000 safety and environmental examinations of foreign vessels entering U.S. ports
- Conducted nearly 4,700 marine casualty investigations
- Performed nearly 7,300 dockside safety examinations
- Issued more than $122 million in state grants and $6.2 million in non-profit grants for boating safety
- Enhanced the ability to detect and locate persons in distress through technology improvements that now cover more than 23,000 miles of the U.S. coastline
- Boarded nearly 3,700 underway fishing vessels to perform safety and compliance checks

Analysis: The above output measurements do not indicate success. Out of the 12,000 safety inspections, how many ships were found to be unsafe and how many unsafe conditions were corrected? How many lives were saved by non-profit grants for boating safety? Measurements showing how many activities were conducted or performed does not indicate success or failure. Without additional numbers to compare against, these Function activities have no real meaning in terms of results.

Outcome Measures (Performance):

- Search and rescue cases saved more than 4,000 lives
- Saved almost $158 million in property
- Issued nearly 84,000 credentials to qualified merchant mariners, who ensure the safe, secure, and efficient navigation of ships carrying 2.6 billion tons of commerce through our nation's ports and waterways

Analysis: The above Outcome Measures describe results. The Coast Guard saved 4,000 lives and $158 million in property. The third measurement is borderline and needs to be rewritten from a results-oriented point-of-view. In fact, these Outcome Measures require additional information as to whether the numbers have improved or not. Of course, lower numbers could be reflecting success as a result of safety training or ship inspections. It is important to look beyond the initial numbers and ask, "What does this mean?" If asking this question receives the answer, "I don't know what this means," then certainly additional analysis is required.

Security:

Output Measures (Function):

- Conducted more than 1,500 security boardings of high interest vessels bound for the United States
- Deployed six patrol boats and 400 personnel to protect Iraq's maritime oil infrastructure, trained Iraqi naval forces, and enforced U.N. sanctions in the Arabian Gulf
- Provided waterside security and escorts for nearly 500 military freight conveyances, which provided supplies to support Operation Iraqi Freedom and Operation Enduring Freedom

Analysis: These are certainly important Functions but they do not report on results. What was the result of the 1,500 security boardings, the Iraq deployment, or escort services? These numbers beg the question again, "What do they mean?"

Outcome Measures (Performance):

- Broke last year's record by removing nearly 185 tons of cocaine bound toward the United States via the transit zone

- Interdicted nearly 5,000 undocumented migrants attempting to illegally enter the United States

Analysis: Removing 185 tons of cocaine certainly demonstrates a positive result in the war against illegal drugs. It would help if the number of undocumented migrants was compared against a previous established baseline. The question is, what constitutes a good number? Are these successes typical or a significant improvement? When looking at these outcomes, you should be able to know what Goals these measures support or justify.

Stewardship:

Output Measures (Function):

- Performed nearly 17,000 facility safety inspections and 20,000 container inspections

- Conducted more than 5,600 fisheries conservation boardings

- Investigated almost 4,000 pollution incidents

Analysis: What was the result of the 17,000 safety inspections? If all 17,000 revealed no safety problems, then maybe such inspections should be cut back. Whereas, if a significant number of serious safety infractions were found, then maybe the number of inspections needs to be increased. Results-oriented numbers can improve and help direct an organization's effectiveness and management of its resources. It can also justify the need for increased funding.

Outcome Measures (Performance):

- Serviced nearly 42,000 aids-to-navigation (such as beacons and buoys) and corrected more than 10,000 discrepancies

- Delivered the first U.S. aid (more than 30 tons of supplies) to the Republic of Georgia following the South Ossetia war

- Rescued citizens and helped restore the marine transportation system during and after Hurricanes Ike and Gustav

- Performed domestic icebreaking, keeping waterways open for commercial traffic and assisting 680 ice transits that carried more than $2 billion worth of cargo

Analysis: By now, you should be able to understand the difference. Correcting 10,000 discrepancies in navigation aids is a good thing, although a better description or criteria of the seriousness of these discrepancies would help. How many citizens were rescued? Some items lack numbers and could use more details regarding impact. What was the positive result by restoring the marine transportation system? What impact (lives saved) resulted in delivering aid to the Republic of Georgia? The answers to these questions could influence Coast Guard funding.

More government examples of Outcome (Result) over Output (Function):

- Instead of increasing vessel inspections and certifications, the Coast Guard began training entry-level crew members to reduce human error in the towing industry. The fatality rate dropped from 91 to 27 for every 100,000 employees.

Analysis: Using training to reduce fatalities is obviously working and clearly justifies the resources. Fewer deaths equates to a safer environment and improved productivity. That's a great success story.

- Instead of counting the forecasts it made, the National Weather Service now measures the warning time given to the public before severe weather. The lead time before tornadoes increased from seven minutes to nine minutes.

  Analysis: If you live in tornado alley, which is more important to you, the number of forecasts or the early warning of a tornado? The ultimate result to be achieved is saving lives from weather disasters. Changing focus from forecasts to saving lives certainly changes an organization's attitude from conducting a Function (counting forecasts) to a Mission (saving lives). That has to make a positive impact on an organization's planning.

- Instead of tracking the response time to questions about veterans' eligibility for burial on its grounds, the National Cemetery System is improving the burial schedule with a Goal to finalize a date within two hours of receiving a request.

  Analysis: You have a deceased warrior. Nothing is worse than waiting for someone to make a scheduling decision during the peak of bereavement. Changing from a Function (tracking response time) to a Mission (finalize schedule) that helps the bereaved (customer) aligns the organization with its customers and their needs.

The above examples demonstrate the difference between Function and Outcome Performance. A shoeshine owner has immediate feedback as to whether the customer is happy or not. Repeat customers demonstrate a satisfaction with an organization's service. Measuring the customers' satisfaction indicates either growing success or impending failure.

More Examples of Performance Goals/Objectives (i.e., PRMs):

- Improve crop productivity using early detection methods to reduce pests by reducing top-ten threat species over next two years by 5%
- Reduce food-borne illnesses by 8% over a 12-month period
- Protect environmentally-important acres by adding 10,000 acres into protective custody
- Increase jobs in distressed communities by 15% of net new jobs
- Reduce patient-waiting time for lab results from 5 days to 2 days
- Increase high school students' readiness for college to 85%
- Reduce vaccine-preventable diseases by 25% in target areas
- Reduce HIV-related deaths by 1,200 cases per year
- Reduce infant deaths by 27 cases a month
- Decrease obesity rates for children from 8% to 5%
- Reduce gun-related violent crimes by 32%
- Reduce acidic water in acid-sensitive regions by 8 cases per year
- Reduce fatal crashes by 21% over next holiday
- Reduce speed-related fatal crashes by 25 percent

Analysis: I cannot stress enough that the numbers should have some basis. These are good measurements providing that the organizations are committed to achieving these numbers. And these numbers must be changed if future analysis indicates changes to the original assumptions.

Another way of looking at measurements:

Planning Commission's Building Inspection Department - Number of:

Input: Building inspectors and permit requests.

Output: Inspections performed, permits issued, and violations cited.

Outcome: Safety issues corrected.

Result: Fewer people injured or killed by structural defects.

NOTE: It is important to point out the adjectives used to describe Performance. Words such as improve, reduce, increase, decrease, expand, etc., are followed by actions. The Performance adjective describes the measurement for success or failure in achieving the action.

Problem with Statistics: An important question with PRMs is what number represents success? Many times a number or percentage is arbitrarily chosen without any basis or analysis to justify the number. Generally, an organization's Goal to reduce something negative or improve something positive (e.g., reduce a disease or improve recovery) cannot be focused on a certain number or percentage without some previous number to compare against. If an organization has increased customers by 5% over the past 14 months, continuing the effort should provide another 5% improvement over the next 14 months, providing that the circumstances have not changed and that the potential customer base is large enough. If the first 5% were people who were ready to become customers, the next 5% may come from a pool of customers less inclined to buy your product, and therefore, may be harder to increase customers over the same time period. It may require a different marketing strategy and schedule to get the second 5%.

Strategic Planning Demystified

Performance Measures require the same careful analysis as the effort to identify the Strategic Plan's Goals, Objectives, and Strategies. An organization needs to conduct market or customer surveys, look at the success or failure of similar efforts, and gather as much available information on the customer's use of the product. From this research comes the analysis of identifying realistic measurements and targets that define success.

I once had an analyst indicate that a contributor had increased electronic submissions by 100%. Sounded impressive until I looked at the data and found that the previous transaction reporting period showed only one electronic submission and the current reporting period showed two submissions, a 100% increase. As impressive as the increase suggested, it didn't mean anything because the client's manual submissions were still in the tens of thousands. The story's lesson is to be careful with statistics and what they suggest. You really need to dig into the minutia to understand what the numbers represent.

In another instance, an organization's average processing time seemed high. It turned out that rejected submissions were held in an error queue and when the error queue was purged, the time held in the error queue was included with normal transaction averages, resulting in an exaggerated, longer, and inaccurate average-processing time. After isolating the error queue data, the data provided a more accurate and improved picture of the system's performance for the customers.

The Department of Justice at one time established for the National Instant Criminal Background Check System a Performance Goal to increase the number of felons found to be attempting to purchase a weapon. The only way I could see the government influencing this number would be to persuade felons to go out and buy weapons using their real identities. The measurement made no sense because the government had no control or influence on the measurement. The statistic simply revealed how many stupid felons had forgotten that they were prohibited from buying a gun legally. The measurement sounded good but it was useless unless the government had a program to encourage felons to buy guns (which it did not).

Trend/Baseline Analysis: Another value of PRMs is the ability to identify trends. Certainly in measuring Functions, organizations usually measure current productivity (trend) against past productivity (baseline) in order to forecast future productivity, particularly when productivity is driven by customer demand.

The US Coast Guard stopping 5,000 undocumented migrants could be a good or bad number, depending on past performance. If past performance averaged 10,000 undocumented migrants, then the 5,000 number could indicate success in discouraging illegal immigration or that illegal immigrants were more successful in avoiding capture. The US Coast Guard needs to determine what the 5,000 number really means.

Most organizations know how to gather statistics (e.g., widgets sold, customers served, unit costs, profits). Most statistics are gathered on a calendar or fiscal basis (e.g., how many widgets sold during the fiscal year's first quarter). In some instances, however, such statistics may not produce the best trend analysis.

There was once a daily chart containing an average of the transactions processed during the month. The totals were divided by the number of days to give a daily average for the month. The first day of the month was an average of one day. On the tenth day, the total transactions for ten days was divided by ten to give a daily average. On the last day of the month, the average would be the total transactions divided by the total days in the month. On the first day of the next month, the statistical chart started over.

The chart contained the averages compiled for each day. Early in the month, there was a wide variance between each day. As the chart line approached the end of the month, the line became more stable. As more data was collected during the month the data became less influenced by occasional anomalies, such as fewer transactions on weekends and holidays. These daily averages were meaningless until the end of the month. The supervisors could not explain how the chart helped to manage transactions, personnel, etc. The chart had been conducted for decades and management assumed someone must have needed the chart.

A calendar month of data (with a variable range of 28 to 31 days, four or five weekends, snow days, and various holidays) had no real chance of identifying an actual trend. The chart was changed to a rolling average to provide management with a real trend analysis. The chart covered the most recent 90 days. Each day, the oldest day was dropped; the current day was added; and the 90 days were averaged. The resulting chart provided a stable and meaningful average. Over time, average transactions began to increase, indicating to management an increase in customer usage. Over time the daily transactions increased from 40K to 60K. This justified technology upgrades to meet increasing daily transactions. There are additional discussions in Part Seven and Appendix D concerning the rolling analysis.

Another example of looking deeper into the statistics concerns stolen identities. The Federal Trade Commission (FTC) reported in 2010 that 11 million identities were stolen. Certainly a frightening number but is it really the right number? Computer databases are continually being hacked with millions of records stolen, but how many stolen identities are used by the bad guys? The FTC received about 370,000 identity theft complaints in 2012. Should we be concerned about the 11 million or the 370,000? Of the billions of data points collected daily by the National Security Agency, how many are seen by an analyst? The lesson learned is to dig deep into the statistics until you know absolutely what number is crucial to the discussion.

When gathering trend statistics, keep an open mind and understand that customer activities may not necessarily be driven by your fiscal calendar. Performance statistics should give you information about customer performance from which you can use to manage your services. Certain calendar events, such as holidays, can affect an organization's activities and can cause short-term changes in a trend analysis. The point I'm making is that an organization should consider non-calendar, non-fixed timeline approaches in identifying PRMs.

Performance Report: Organizations should create and attach a Performance Report to the Strategic Plan that summarizes past performance, lists current measurements and results status, and describes targeted future results. This report reminds management that they must track the Goals and Objectives for success. The PRMs form the basis for the report and should be distributed to components that influence the measurements and who can develop or change strategies to address potential approaching problems. The Performance Report also has a marketing value to stakeholders and customers. Both groups need to know that the organization is successfully meeting the customer's needs.

SUMMARY: PRMs are critical to Strategic Planning. Without good PRMs, you're blind driving down the road. If you can't see your journey's progress, then how do you know if you are on the road to success? Good PRMs require work but the numbers will reveal if you're meeting the customers' requirements. The key is to measure and retrieve the right numbers. Good PRMs will show if the customers are buying or receiving a product of value; if your customer base is expanding; and if future success and growth is happening. For non-profits, PRMs should reveal if the disease is being reduced. For government, PRMs reveal if agencies are achieving the legislative intent.

G. Accountability to the Plan

All organizations have a chain of command and each manager, sub-manager, etc., has a job description detailing their duties. The higher-level manager (HLM) rates the lower-level manager (LLM) based on the LLM's performance in accomplishing the job description's Functions. It is rare, however, that the Strategic Plan's Goals and Objectives are part of this rating system. In addition, most Strategic Plans concern only the executive level with no explanation as to how the planning process tracks down through the organization and LLMs.

To improve the Strategic Plan's performance, an organization must establish a **Chain of Accountability**. **Chart 5** outlines how you drill down through the organization where HLM Goals become LLM's Mission, HLM Objectives become LLM's Goals, etc.

This chain of accountability becomes the basis for a contract between the different management levels. It's like a family tree; everyone is connected. This approach forces each organizational level to pay attention to the plan because each level will be held accountable for their part of the plan. As previously mentioned, accountability is one of the four major requirements for successful planning.

Strategic Planning Demystified

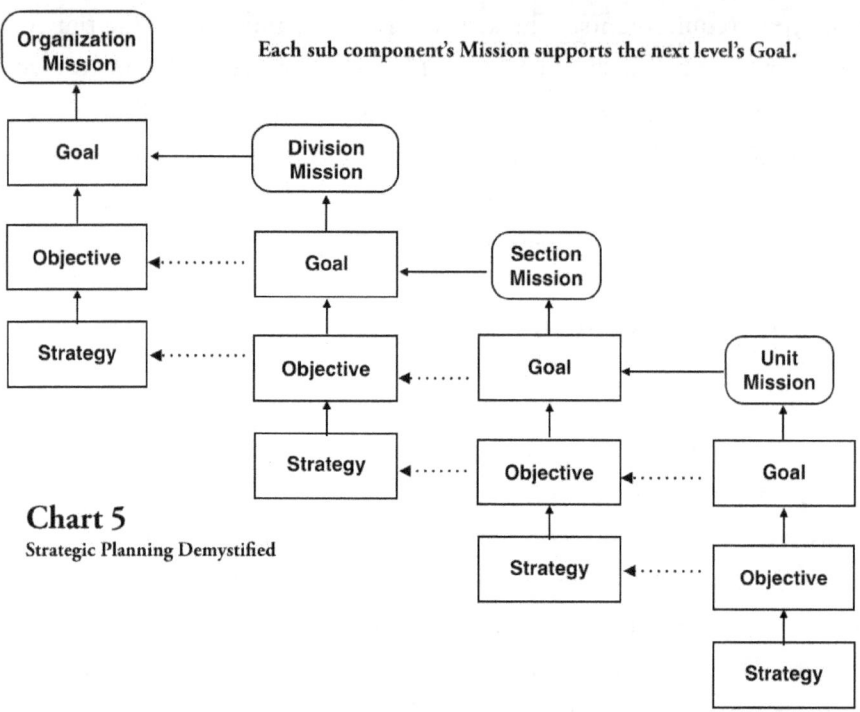

Chart 5
Strategic Planning Demystified

Organizations usually evaluate and rate a manager's job performance against the job description. Most rating systems, however, lack a connection to the organization's Strategic Plan. I suggest a vertical contract between upper and lower managers connected by the organization's Strategic Plan's Goals and Objectives. The contract can be changed when Goals and Objectives change. A manager's performance appraisal should be tied directly to this contract. The contract will cite the planning activities attributed to the manager.

Now, instead of reinventing the wheel, an organization can incorporate this approach within existing work performance reviews. For example, add a paragraph or section to an existing performance appraisal that cites the Goal(s) and/or Objective(s) that the manager will be held accountable.

Strategic Planning Demystified

Several years ago, the U.S. Office of Personnel Management updated the appraisal system in an attempt to connect Senior Executive Service job ratings to the Strategic Plan's performance. The following summarized elements were added:

- Balanced performance measurements that balance organizational results with the perspectives of distinct groups, including customers and employees.

- Specific performance results expected from the executive during the appraisal period, focusing on measurable outcomes from the Strategic Plan or other measurable outputs and outcomes clearly aligned to organizational Goals and Objectives.

- The executive demonstrates a very high level of performance beyond that required for successful performance in the executive's position and scope of responsibilities. The executive is a proven, highly effective leader who builds trust and instills confidence in agency leadership, peers, and employees. The executive consistently exceeds established performance expectations, timelines, or targets, as applicable.

- Advances progress significantly toward achieving one or more strategic Goals.

These same elements can be applied to business or non-profit organizations. These new rules hold government managers accountable and require them to also focus on Performance and not just Function. I observed that managers became serious about Strategic Planning as a result of their job performance assessments being connected to Strategic Planning.

Non-Profit Small Organizations with Volunteers: Small organizations using volunteers can't enforce accountability the way an organization can employ it with a salaried staff. Volunteers actually have the "take it or leave it" position. They will only put the effort that they want to put into an organization. Some volunteers will work hard and can be trusted to accomplish whatever the task. Others will do what they will do.

You've probably been a member of a volunteer organization that has a hundred members but only ten to fifteen members actually conducting the organization's activities. The other members support the organization with their dues or will make an appearance at meetings or bring a pie to the annual fundraiser.

So how do you get commitment and accountability for a non-profit? Here again, clearly stated Mission and Goals are key to keeping volunteers. With written Goals and Objectives, an organization can put together informal contract-type assignment sheets that outline what needs to be done by each volunteer or group of volunteers. Seeing something in writing reinforces the commitment. Written instructions, like a plan, make it clear on what is needed. It also reduces the uncertainty and fear of the unknown.

Volunteer and non-profit organizations usually have several major Objectives to raise funds, recruit volunteers, gain community support, and provide services to the customer. Volunteers need to be assigned a task to support one or more activities.

If an organization's volunteers raise funds to support worthy causes, it is important to track the contributions to ensure they succeed in doing something good. That kind of PRM reinforces the volunteers' belief that they are making a difference. For example, it's not good enough to just donate glasses, money, blood, clothes, etc. The volunteers need to know that someone now has good vision to read, has obtained a job, is now fed, has returned to good health, etc. Did the donated blood save any lives? Does someone now have adequate clothing to make it through the winter? When volunteers see the results of their efforts, they will continue to volunteer. Volunteers' performance also comes from good leadership and the volunteers' inner sense of value and duty to the community.

What inspires you? Does your job, your company, your volunteer activities provide a strong feeling of satisfaction? Do you feel you make a difference? You can only answer these questions when you know that the organization's performance is meeting its Mission and Goals.

SUMMARY: Strategic Planning Demystified approach creates a chain of custody and accountability throughout the organization by connecting the Strategic Plan's Goals, Objectives, and Strategies to specific management positions. This ensures managers will pay attention to the planning process. This accountability can also inspire management and the work force by having clear and understood end-result activities to focus on. Performing activities that have known benefits to the customer provides increased job satisfaction to the organization.

H. Organizational Alignment

Accountability also identifies weaknesses in the organizational structure. When an organization identifies its true Mission, it needs to evaluate its organizational structure to ensure that all components line up to meet the correct Goals and Objectives. In developing Mission, Goals, and Objectives at the different organizational levels, it will become obvious when a component's Goals do not support the next level up.

When this happens, an organization must:

- Relocate the component to another or new part of the organization where it will support a higher-level Goal.

- Amend the Mission or Goal at the next level up to include the component.
- Cease the component's activities.

Support Activities: Most Strategic Plans do not include the indirect and support service Functions, such as personnel, facility maintenance, human resources department, financial unit, etc. Small components that provide support services are usually left out of the plan. Certainly when discussing the organization or agency at the executive level, these secondary Functions usually don't have a major Goal. But somewhere in the lower part of the planning methodology, they should be included. Every Function throughout the organization should be able to show how it directly or indirectly supports the organization at some level and eventually supports the organization's Goals and Mission.

For example, should the Computer Services Unit be located under the component in charge of overall facility management or under the production component? If the Computer Services Unit provides support throughout the organization (production, administrative, facility, customer support, etc.) it might be better managed under the administrative or facility support branch or component. If the Computer Services Unit only supports the Goals and Objectives of the production component, it probably should reside within the production component.

In another example, an organization has a staff that cleans the restrooms. What impact does filthy, unkempt bathrooms have on morale, or what kind of impression does it have on customers? Think of all the indirect and administrative activities within the organization that affect an organization's internal performance. The carpet is dirty and torn. The computers continually crash. Annual leave records are incorrect. These failed Functions can negatively impact other components' efforts to support the Mission, Goals, and Objectives!

Strategic Planning Demystified

I agree that it is difficult to make the connection between administrative and indirect activities with the organization's overall Mission. But understand that there must be a connection, no matter how tenuous. In some cases, however, if no reasonable explanation can be given for an internal activity, it should be discontinued and its resources transferred to efforts that truly support the Mission.

In a small business, this becomes even more crucial because of limited resources. The shoe repair store owner shouldn't be providing any service that does not meet the Mission of "repaired shoes stay repaired." So, selling soft drinks should not be included unless it adds value to the customer. For example, add a Goal or Objective/Strategy that includes, "Improve the customer's experience at the store by providing drinks and snacks when they wait for service."

Some organizations volunteer time or sponsorship to civic projects (fund raisers, sport teams, youth organizations, etc.) as a way of giving back to the community some civic value. We know, however, that even these activities actually are marketing tools to improve branding and image, and therefore, can support marketing Goals or Objectives.

Mission Creep: Finally, a good Strategic Plan inhibits Mission creep. It reveals Functions that do not support the plan or are not incorporated into the plan at the right spot. Organizations frequently add Functions without first determining how such Functions support a Goal or Objective. A manager sees an opportunity for empire building by taking on new activities, even when such activities should not be under that manager. A new Function needs to be placed within the component where it clearly supports a Goal and Objective. The Strategic Planning Demystified approach forces an analysis to determine if, in fact, a new Function should be added and where it belongs in the Strategic Plan and the organization's structure.

Strategic Planning Demystified

SUMMARY: The Strategic Plan's structure is not complicated. It is like a family tree that spreads out as you drill down from grandparents through parents and children and finally to grandchildren. If the organization's Mission, Goals, Objectives, and Strategies are correctly identified and crafted into a short but clearly focused statements, then the supporting lower-level Goals, Objectives, Strategies, and PRMs will clearly support the Mission. The Strategic Plan also validates the organizational structure to ensure that all levels properly support each other.

< >

PART FOUR
STRATEGIC PLANNING COORDINATOR (SPC)

The SPC manages the planning process at a senior level with the authority to command respect and cooperation at all levels of the organization. Ideally, the SPC should work for the most senior executive which will demonstrate the executive's commitment to Strategic Planning. Placing the SPC at a lower organizational level weakens the SPC's ability to achieve a working Strategic Planning process that is taken seriously at all organizational levels.

The SPC has the critical and full-time responsibility to:

- Create and manage the organization's Strategic Planning process.

- Document the organization's Mission, Goals, Objectives, Strategies, PRMs, etc.

- Educate the organization on how the planning process works and where each manager fits within the planning process.

- Initiate and coordinate the planning and analysis tools needed to help the organization to stay on course.

- Review the Mission, Goals, Objectives, and Strategies from all departments to ensure a strong and logical linkage.

- Review performance contracts between managers to ensure they correctly connect to the plan.

- Identify and track the PRMs at the organizational level and help lower-level components identify and track their PRMs.

- Train new executives and employees on the planning process and conduct refresher courses to current employees.

- Change the Strategic Plan when significant events occur that impact the Goals, Objectives, and/or Strategies; disseminate changes to the entire organization; and ensure that the organization adjusts to the changes.
- Nurture a cooperative and collaborative culture between components into a unified and willing participation in the Strategic Planning process.
- Help each component to identify its own Mission, Goals, Objectives, and Strategies that support the Goals, Objectives, and Strategies at the next highest organization level.

The SPC also liaisons with stakeholders to solicit, analyze, communicate, and validate requirements that influence the organization's plans. The SPC should identify problems and opportunities in the context of the requirements and recommend solutions that enable the organization to achieve its Goals.

The SPC can help the organization avoid:
- Unclear business directions.
- Poorly defined, missing, or incomplete business requirements.
- Conflicts between internal components.
- False assumptions.

In addition to the SPC, each department, section, branch, etc., should have its own SPC who liaisons directly with the organization's SPC. This is not necessarily a full-time position but is a senior-level person high enough within a component to: 1) provide solid planning and performance information, 2) perform SPC duties within his or her component, 3) liaison with the senior SPC.

Ultimately, the SPCs ensure that the Strategic Planning process works and doesn't fade away or become out-of-date. With leadership's support and protection, the SPCs make the Strategic Planning process a valuable and worthwhile effort.

Although this book provides guidance on how to plan, the SPC makes it happen using the skill and ability to work with management and supervisors to draw out what really counts.

The SPC requires:

- Excellent analytical skills.
- Clear understanding of Strategic Planning.
- A creative mind to identify, initiate, and conduct good PRMs.
- Good observation skills.
- Excellent people skills.
- The ability to draw out information from people in a constructive manner.
- Good plain-language writing skills.
- Good oral communications skills.

When meeting with components, management, stakeholders, and customers, the SPC should perform in the following manner:

- Listen and learn through effective written and verbal exchanges to surface the important information
- Perform as a neutral party and allow different ideas to be considered
- Examine and analyze the retrieved information
- Probe ideas and guide management using questions

- Provide encouragement throughout the process
- Mentor participants in planning
- Keep the business focused on the customer

Contractor Support: An optional approach to having a SPC employee is to hire a contractor. This will require a competitive contract solicitation process to ensure you contract the right person and company. Be sure the contract includes training the organization's employee(s) who take over planning after the contract is completed. Missing this requirement will result in a short-term planning effort with no long-term effectiveness.

SUMMARY: The SPC makes Strategic Planning happen by coordinating the organization's planning activities at all organizational levels. By having a coordinated planning effort, management will have available the important information that is needed to make informed decisions for the organization's future. Finally, the person assigned to the SPC position must have unique communication skills to draw out and interpret the right information needed for planning.

< >

PART FIVE
UNDERSTANDING RISK AND FAILURE

> **Failure:** Not attaining a desired or intended result or outcome, resulting in harm to the customer and/or organization.
>
> **Risk:** An internal or external unplanned event that could negatively impact an organization's effort to achieve success.
>
> **Calculated Risk:** A recognized risk in which an organization is willing to consider taking in an effort to achieve success.

Strategic Planning requires an understanding and analysis of any potential risk and/or failure. Generally, a risk is an internal or external event that may have a negative impact on an organization. A risk can sometimes be anticipated (changing market demand) while other events can blindside an organization (unforeseen natural disaster). Recognizing risk is important to all organizations. If you can see a growing risk early, you have the opportunity to counter or reduce its negative impact.

Failure, on the other hand, is the flip side of success. All organizations try to avoid failure because failure can weaken or end the Mission. Recognizing potential failure provides a strong incentive to create a plan that avoids failure. I have worked under these conditions and it can be very motivating knowing that the grim reaper is at your heels. For that reason, it is important to discuss both risk and failure. Part of the analysis to identify Goals, Objectives, and Strategies should include the identification of a potential risk or failure. Failure describes what happens when an organization fails its Mission. Failure falls under the following two categories.

1. **Events that an organization has the ability to control and avoid.**
   Examples would be:

   - Poorly managed inventory.
   - Product defects.
   - Poor customer service.
   - High employee attrition rate because of poor pay/benefits.
   - No backup or alternate plan to cover loss of supplier or support.
   - Vehicle break downs resulting in poor delivery performance.

2. **Events that are beyond the organization's control.**
   Examples would be:

   - Unforeseen natural events (e.g., hurricane, flood, tornado, civil unrest, terrorist event).
   - Negative legislation causing insurmountable regulatory obstacles
   - Economic downturn beyond anyone's expectations
   - Unexpected change in customer demand or requirements

The above failures were risks before becoming failures. That is why it is critical to recognize risks early, before they become failures. It does seem obvious and yet organizations find themselves failing when everyone around the event knew the risk but didn't act to avoid the risk from becoming a failure. Some people recognized the impending housing bubble and the pyramid-scheme-like profile of derivatives in the early 2000s but Wall Street and government "experts" refused to recognize or even consider the risks and potential financial failures. Climate change may prove to be another example.

We know that obesity (risk) kills people (failure). People who recognize and change an unhealthy lifestyle can lower the risk of early death (failure) and live a longer, prosperous, and healthier life (success). Having a Mission to save lives by reducing obesity recognizes that failing the Mission will result in deaths. Death represents failure which keeps the organization energized and focused on saving lives (success).

A hospital recognizes that a contagious disease can be disastrous to its Mission. It needs a Contingency Plan that will checkmate a dangerous disease from spreading through the hospital. Nothing is worse than recognizing failure but doing nothing until it's too late.

Recognizing and adapting to changing technologies can reduce the risk of complacency and of losing market share. Look at all the computer companies that have come and gone. For some reason, they failed to track market trends, technology advancements, etc. At some point, these companies failed the customer, lost their market, crushed by competition, and went out of business.

Issues to be Considered:

- Recognizing potential failure provides an organization the opportunity to avoid or reduce failure.

- Successful risk management stops serious mistakes before they can occur and eliminates or minimizes potential financial, market, and/or branding losses.

- Understanding the potential impact of failure (to the organization, the stakeholder, and, most importantly, to the organization's customer) is key to avoiding such failure. Management can use this knowledge to justify the effort needed to achieve the Mission. Controlling risk to avoid failure must be recognized and addressed somewhere in the plan. If a cost overrun or schedule slippage begins to occur, management needs to take immediate, corrective action to reduce or avoid the negative event.

- Identifying, understanding, and describing failure can explain why a government or non-profit organization needs funding or resources. If a funding source is told that the Mission is to educate people about diabetes, it is easy for that funding source to say no. But if the request clearly shows that funding will result in fewer people dying of diabetes, it becomes harder for the funding source to say no.

- Though the excitement of achieving a meaningful Mission provides incentive for staff and others to work for success, the fear of failure can also provide an equally strong incentive to work harder for success. If Goals are accomplished, customers will buy more product and the business prospers. If Goals fail, the customer stops buying product and the company goes out of business. You lose your job. Understanding and enumerating the impact of failure to the organization provides a strong incentive to do all that is possible to avoid failure and to achieve success.

- The better the Mission, the higher the risk of failure. Building an electric car that travels more than 500 miles-per-charge with a full recharge time of 3 minutes would bring fantastic success. The risk of failure can be high because the dependency on gasoline fueled vehicles is still strong and developing a 3 minute recharge, 500-mile battery will be technically difficult. So, a good Mission Statement will suggest that failing the Mission will result in a significant failure for the organization and its customers.

- One risk can be quick "success." There was once a television advertisement showing people initiating a new Internet company. In the first few minutes, they received several orders for their product. They were excited. A few minutes later, they had several hundred orders. Now they were really ecstatic. Then the orders began to arrive exponentially from hundreds to thousands. Suddenly, they realized that they were swamped with orders far beyond their capability to deliver. They failed to understand the potential risk of an Internet market. They failed to plan for success.

- Some future failures are beyond an organization's control, such as economic, political, weather, technological, etc. Events like 9/11, hurricanes, earth quakes, economic recession, etc., provide strong examples of failures beyond an organization's control. Many companies disappeared or failed because of catastrophes beyond their control. But even for some of these events, organizations could have developed contingencies, backup plans, or "what if" scenarios. Understanding and creating backup plans is a clear recognition of potential risks which an organization can plan to avoid or at least to reduce the impact.

- Risk assessment also reduces complacency. Although an organization has been successful in the past, complacency can allow unidentified risks to weaken an organization, causing it to lose its competitiveness and successfulness.

The tools to identify failure or risk are discussed in Part Seven, *Analysis*, where some methodologies discuss ways to identify emerging risks and failures. What constitutes failure varies with each organization. What must be remembered is the need to identify potential risks and failures as soon as possible and evaluate their impact to the organization's effort to succeed. The sooner a risk and/or failure is identified, the sooner action can be taken to avoid it.

I once analyzed a new contract using a process called Earned Value. It compares the actual expenditure of cost, schedule, and work against the planned cost, schedule, and work outlined in the contract. After analyzing the first three months of the contract's performance, Earned Value disclosed that the contractor was heading toward a significant cost and schedule overrun. My analysis was given to upper management but they were overconfident that the contractor could make up for these deficiencies. In time, however, it became apparent that the contractor was quickly failing. Once the contractor's poor performance became blatantly obvious, actions were taken to repair the contract. The project manager was replaced and eventually the contractor completed the task, although the cost and schedule slipped by millions of dollars and several years.

The problem was that management refused to acknowledge the growing risk and did not want to share bad news with its senior management. Never be afraid of bad news when it appears early enough where action can be taken to manage it. The sooner a potential risk or failure is identified, the sooner actions can be taken to prevent or reduce its impact. Never be afraid to find failure or identify risks.

In another contract, I observed again where Earned Value began indicating schedule and cost increases, except this time the manager pulled back unnecessary features, reigned in spending, and paid closer attention to the contractor's performance. As a result, the project came in on time and on budget.

Calculated Risk: A calculated risk is an uncertain venture in which an organization is willing to take a risky course of action to achieve success. Companies conduct calculated risks all the time. The word "calculated" indicates that the risk has been analyzed and found to be acceptable. Investing in the stock market would be a good example.

The International Organization for Standardization (ISO) 31000 defines risk as "the effect of uncertainty on objectives." Because risk is directly linked to Objectives, it suggests that risk is not inherently "bad." If risk can be managed effectively, opportunities can be exploited. Risk is generated by every decision that an organization makes.

The ISO helps to reconcile risk management processes in existing and future standards. It provides a common approach in dealing with specific risks. A Risk Management Plan analysis should be part of the Strategic Planning Process.

SUMMARY: Understanding risk and failure is critical to preventing future problems. It also provides the incentive and justification for taking actions that can lead to success. The Strategic Plan should describe the risks and failures that have been identified and what actions will be taken if they occur.

< >

PART SIX
TACTICAL PLAN

> **Short-term planning in which activities and resources have been identified and committed.**

A Strategic Plan needs a Tactical Plan. The Tactical Plan can be synonymous with an Action, Project, Compartment, Department, or Program Plan. With a small, emerging, or new company, it could also be similar to the Business Plan. How many Tactical Plans an organization requires will depend on the organization's size and complexity. The Tactical Plan(s) should be attached to or at least referenced within the Strategic Plan's appropriate Strategy Section. The top of the Tactical Plan hierarchy connects directly to the Strategies at the bottom of the organization's Strategic Plan's hierarchy.

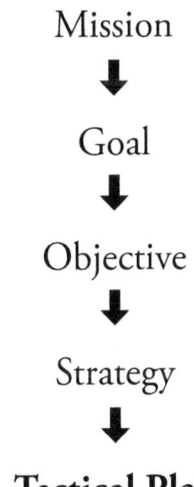

Organization's Strategic Plan

Mission
⬇
Goal
⬇
Objective
⬇
Strategy
⬇
Tactical Plan

A Tactical Plan lays out the specific actions needed for achieving the Strategic Plan's Strategies. In fact, the organization's early Strategies most likely generated the Tactical Plans for each major component. Each department develops and executes a Tactical Plan which lists the planned activities needed to be accomplished. As each department executes its Tactical Plan, it generates or supports the organization's overall success. Poorly performing Strategic Plans usually are the result of failures at the Tactical level. Having a good Tactical Plan will clearly differentiate between successful or unsuccessful Strategic Planning.

- Tactical Plans are created by various organizational departments: production, operations, marketing, sales, development, technology, administration, facilitation, etc.

- Tactical Plans describe what the departments will accomplish and detail the required activities, schedules, and resources.

- Each component will have a designated SPC to manage and coordinate the Tactical Plan.

After the organization's Strategic Plan has been drafted but before it is finalized, each component should ensure that its own Tactical Plan will support the new or updated strategic direction of the company. If a conflict arises as to what can or cannot be accomplished by a department, negotiation must take place to either amend the Strategic Plan or to find a way for the department to accomplish its part of the Strategic Plan.

Tactical Planning for Large Organizations: Most large organizations most likely have some form of Tactical Planning for each component that supports the overall Strategic Plan. I would suggest using existing low-level plans to connect to the Strategic Plan.

Tactical Planning for Small Organizations: For small organizations, the Tactical Plan may be represented by the Strategic Plan's Strategies. In some cases, an organization's Action or Business plans may detail the specific actions needed to be taken for achieving the Strategies. For the very small business, I would skip the Tactical Plan and use what ever daily activity planning method that works for the business. In most cases, a to-do list will be sufficient, as long as it supports the Mission and Goals.

Tactical Planning Elements: At the top of the Tactical Plan you have the Tactical Goal(s) which is the same as a Strategic Plan's Strategy or a more finely tuned descriptive action to support a Strategic Plan's Strategy. Each Tactical Goal will have the following parts:

- **Link:** Describes the Strategic Plan's Strategy item being supported.
- **Results:** What is to be achieved. It could be expressed as a PRM, an improvement to the customer, or a positive change in the organization's environment.
- **Activities:** What needs to happen.
- **Schedule:** A start-to-finish timeline showing when activities will take place.
- **Resources:** A list of the cost, personnel, facility, technology, expertise, etc., with a link to the schedule.

The Tactical level identified resources will provide the total resource numbers required at the Strategic Planning level. In this instance, "resource" can refer to all costs and measurable elements associated with the activity. Activities and schedule have their own part.

Activity, schedule, and resource categories influence each other. The amount of effort to accomplish an activity influences the schedule and resource. In turn, the schedule may influence the activity and resource factors. And of course, resource influences activity and schedule.

Aspects to be considered:

- Activities, schedules, and resources have certain limits that affect each other. If you need a new computer program for your technology, you need to know how many lines of code a programmer can write and how long it will take. The schedule may require the programming to be completed in one year. If programming by one programmer will take three years, the project will need three or more programmers to finish programming in one year. If you only have funding for two programmers, then it will take longer than one year. No one said that planning is easy.

- Activities, schedules, and resources may need to be broken down into sub-parts for complex projects or activities. Large organizations could have a Tactical Plan for each major component within a company. In fact, most large organizations should already have Tactical Plans in place which align with the organization's Strategic Plan.

- Small organizations have fairly basic activities, schedules, and resources. The areas that are usually missed are the indirect or overhead resources and activity requirements that sneak up to consume a schedule. A home remodeler might estimate a kitchen upgrade's schedule to be two days until he finds a rotten floor requiring a longer schedule and more resources.

Other Planning Documents: Some organizations have existing planning documents. When possible, use them in lieu of creating a new Tactical Plan. I would suggest either:

- Referencing the existing planning document in the Strategic Plan,
- Retitling the existing planning document as the Tactical Plan, or

- Combining the existing plan with the new Tactical Plan.

Examples of plans an organization might already have:

- Action Plan
- Business Plan
- Marketing Plan
- Enterprise Plan
- Technology Plan
- Production Plan
- Enterprise Architecture Plan

At this point, an in-depth discussion on all the details found within a Tactical Plan would require its own book. What you need to understand is that the Tactical Plan should be general enough to provide direction to weekly or monthly activities but specific enough to show upper management what must be done to accomplish the Strategic Plan.

One last thought. Different components within a large organization must have access to each other's Tactical Plans. This will help avoid conflicts by understanding activities that are needed or affected by each other's activities. The organization's SPC has the responsibility to review all planning documents to ensure they all properly connect. In business, we call this Configuration Management. I once observed a component insert a project for Internet connectivity as an Objective. Once they accomplished the Objective, they sent the project to the technical component to manage the program. The technical people said no, they were unaware of the other component's project and it was not included in their Technical Plan, and therefore, they would not manage it. If they had read each other's part of the Strategic Plan, they could have resolved the disconnect in the beginning (avoided failure).

Strategic Planning Demystified

SUMMARY: You set forth a Mission to improve your home environment by building a new home. You hire an architect to draw up plans to your specifications. At this point you have a Strategic Plan. But without a contractor and subcontractors to execute the plan, the new home won't be built. The project requires a foundation, framing, roofing, plumbing, electrical, etc. The contractor provides comprehensive work orders outlining the activities, schedules, and resources required to build the home. These work orders represent the Tactical Plan. From the blueprints, the contractor and subcontractors can coordinate their activities so that everything fits together as planned.

Unfortunately, most Strategic Planning efforts end at the time the Strategic Planning document is published. Without a Tactical Plan to implement the long-term strategies, it is not likely the Strategic Plan will accomplish anything.

< >

PART SEVEN
ANALYSIS

> **Good analysis is key to successful planning.**

Generally, an organization begins Strategic Planning by obtaining ideas and proposals from senior managers as to where the organization needs to go. That's fine but it also helps to analyze your customer's current state of affairs in relation to your organization's goods and/or services. From there, you can determine reasonable future projections, requirements, and/or directions for the organization.

A good analysis provides the following information needed to formulate Goals, Objectives, and Strategies.

- Customer satisfaction and future needs
- Actions needed to improve the product for the customer
- Available information, facts, and experiences regarding the organization and its customers
- "Best-guess" estimates for facts that are not yet available or don't yet exist but need to be projected or estimated
- Reasonable estimation on the activities, schedules, and resources needed to get from here to the future
- Competition's challenges and deciding what you can do better
- Validating assumptions
- Potential risks and/or failures
- Stakeholders' input
- Critically review all things

An analysis would include topics, such as:

- Customer trends and requirements
- Product development
- Market
- Sales
- Finances
- Competition
- Resources
- Technology
- Manufacturing
- Regulations
- Management
- Stakeholders
- Environment (add your own adjective, e.g., business environment)

Successfully analyzing the future relies on the skill of the person or group conducting the analysis. The organization must also have the nerve, energy, and will to make drastic or difficult decisions based upon the analysis knowing the risk of being wrong.

One aspect of analysis is the recognition that some information is just not available or does not exist. Missing information can be information in itself. The absence of information concerning some aspect of the market might reveal an unidentified risk or opportunity. In the absence of information, the analysis can insert "place holders" or a best-guess, intelligent, and reasonable assumption to form a basis from which other conclusions and strategies can be formulated, contingent that the actual information will eventually become available. An organization, however, must be careful not to base too much on "place holders" because if they are drastically wrong, failure can be quick and complete.

To reduce the uncertainty, an organization must make as thorough an analysis as possible. In the beginning of this book I discussed indicators as to when Strategic Plans may not be as successful as they should be. Using that approach, an analysis may not be as successful when the staff or management:

- Does not have the experience to assess today's environment and to project the future.

- Only uses at-hand information without taking the effort to seek out additional information.

- Only focuses on the most positive spin on future growth with little or no analysis or discussion concerning risks.

- Does not ask, "Where should we be going for the customer and how do we get there?"

- Focuses on the organization's Functions and not on the customer requirements.

- Limits themselves into an artificial time period, such as a "Five-Year Plan," where they either stretch out or squeeze in projections into five years. What appears to be a logical approach is actually a cop out to avoid the difficult task of a real analysis. On some TV home renovation shows, novice renovators base their renovation schedule on the time they can give to the project rather than the time it really takes to renovate a kitchen or bathroom. Invariably they experience schedule and cost overruns and in some cases project failure.

And what is most important to realize is that today's analysis, no matter how good, has a tendency over time to get off track. Strategic Planning needs to have an ongoing analysis process. As the organization moves into the future, it gains new information and experience that can update and realign the plan to keep it on track or to change course, if needed. Unfortunately, most Strategic Planning efforts are one-night-stands with no ongoing mechanism to evaluate and amend the plan as needed. Whereas, a good Strategic Plan is like a successful marriage, continually improving and adjusting with age.

When a significant and unplanned event occurs (e.g., economic recession, natural disaster, new technology), organizations immediately evaluate the impact. Organizations usually do not wait for some future date to assess the impact of an event on organizational Goals. Unforeseen events cause organizations to immediately change Goals and reassign resources. I suspect, however, that some organizations fail to conduct an orderly planning process to figure out what the true impact will be and what needs to be done. They have a knee-jerk response by adding new levels of bureaucracy (e.g., Dept. of Homeland Security) or throwing funding to components without a real plan based on a sound analysis that would show how best to respond. This especially occurs in organizations that do not have an ongoing planning process.

So, how do you conduct an analysis? You need to go through a thinking process in which you ask as many questions as possible regarding the organization's product and the customer's requirement. Research includes where society and the customer are going in relation to the organization. Analysis includes talking to outside groups that influence or affect the organization. These groups include stakeholders, regulators, suppliers, retailers, and customers. At this point, let's look at the elements of the analysis.

A. Elements of an Analysis:

What should be analyzed?

- **Past Performance:** Provides a strong indicator of how or if the organization has been meeting or approaching the Mission, Goals, and Objectives. Past Performance provides the baseline from which current Performance is measured against.

- **Current Performance:** Evaluates the organization's current performance. Is the organization on target with current Goals, Objectives, and Strategies?

- **Future Performance:** Analyze the future by asking questions, e.g.:
  - What are the current trends in business, non-profit activity, government policy regarding customer requirements, the economy, technology, etc.?
  - What do today's trends say about your product and customer?
  - Where is the competition going? Do you follow, lead, or take a different path?
  - What are the customers' future expectations or requirements?
  - Can you do more or better for the customer?

  Once information has been gathered, an organization can begin formulating reasonable and educated estimates on attainable, future Performances. What is important to stress regarding future assumptions is the need for continuing analysis to validate or change assumptions.

- **Dependencies:** Identify external and internal components that an organization relies upon for support. Recognizing and being aware of dependencies reduces risk. External dependencies would be suppliers, funding sources, infrastructure support (transportation, utilities, etc.)

government regulations, technologies, economics, social demographics, etc. Internal components would be an organization's facility maintenance, administrative (personnel, purchasing, etc.) or other components not directly involved with the product but essential to managing and supporting the product.

- **Stakeholder:** A stakeholder is a person or organization that has a stake in the organization's success. Examples of stakeholders would be stock holders, creditors, suppliers, retailers, investors, employees, etc. Said another way, someone who may benefit or suffer as a result of the organization's success or failure.

  Another Stakeholder type would be people who provide financial support, such as donors or taxpayers. When a person donates money or materials to a charitable organization, they expect their support will help an organization's targeted recipients. Taxpayers expect the government to deliver government services that benefit society (and maybe themselves).

- **Customer**: The person or entity that ultimately benefits from an organization's product. If customers are happy, they will buy or use more and will recommend the organization to others. Citizens who are pleased with the government services will believe that their taxes were well spent. Therefore, an organization must monitor the customer's success in using its product to ensure that it has been successful. Customer satisfaction represents the most important Performance Measurement. The ultimate result of conducting a good analysis is setting Goals that will meet the customer's current and/or future requirements or expectations.

  Part of the analysis will also help to develop a marketing strategy. Identifying how to reach the right customer with your product can be just as important as identifying the customer's requirements. Having a treatment for diabetes is worth nothing if you don't connect with diabetics.

- **Resources/Activities:** An organization must identify and list the resources and activities needed to achieve success. Resources would include funding, staffing, facility and logistical support, technology, training, product or service development, production/manufacturing, materials and supplies, overhead and indirect costs, income, profit, or other identifiable resource.

Most plans fail to include an analysis that identifies the activities needed to accomplish the Goals and Objectives. Without this analysis, planning for future Goals and Objectives has to be difficult. How can an organization cite a Goal without knowing the effort, time, and cost needed to accomplish the Goal?

Once you've identified customer requirements, you must then identify what activities need to be taken. Next, an organization determines what resources are needed and if those resources will be available. If yes, then it can proceed with some confidence. If resources are lacking, it can either make a stronger case for funding the Goal, or amend or withdraw the Goal.

Conservative Statistical Approach: When measuring an organization's success, some studies will stretch or exaggerate the measurement in order to report the best number. I suggest leaning towards a conservative approach when gathering statistics to justify or document success. Why? You want your Performance Measurement to withstand scrutiny and review. If someone else measures your organization's performance, you want their measurement to be equal to or better than your own statistic. Nothing presents problems more than conflicting statistical results that suggest that the organization's performance has been less successful than documented. You want solid statistics that can be stated as being potentially better than reported. It gives the statistics more credibility and instills stronger confidence in the statistics.

In addition, you should obtain the biggest sample as possible. It might take more time and resources, but the larger the sampling, the more accurate the indicated results. In fact, tabulating all the available data provides the most accurate analysis. Rather than sampling every ten customers, try sampling all customers. In today's technology environment, organizations can sample all customers electronically.

Small Business Approach: For a small business, and in particular a sole proprietorship, this discussion of analysis can be overwhelming. Don't over think the process. Buy a pad of sticky-notes and write your primary business activities on them. Activities can be broken down into key categories as to what needs to be done. For example,

- Single activities needed to create the business
- Activities for creating and producing the product
- Marketing the product
- Selling the product
- Other activities needed to run the business

Place the notes on a wall in a logical order of events. This is called a Gantt or Project Chart. It helps you visualize what needs to be done. Once these key activities are on the wall, your grasp on the situation becomes clearer. Now you should note the estimated time and cost it will take to accomplish these activities. Put notes indicating periods of time above the activity notes to give you a timeline of events. It really doesn't matter if you are starting a shoe repair store or running a multi-million company. Charting your journey is like a sailor marking a navigation chart with waypoints to ensure that the journey is successfully completed and avoids possible obstacles.

B. The Analyst

A skilled analyst is empowered to analyze and to make statements and projections based upon the best available facts and assumptions. Besides using the tools described throughout this book, an analyst:

- Conducts independent thinking.
- Takes a long view of issues or processes.
- Does not accept "business as usual" thinking.

Educated assumptions can be made when sufficient facts have been considered. An analyst must also have good writing and verbal skills to clearly communicate and convey an analysis in a manner that is understandable and convincing to the audience. The analyst should also have the same qualities that were outlined for the SPC cited early in the book. Each major program within a large organization should have an experienced and qualified analyst(s).

C. Analysis Tools

There are many and different analytical approaches available to help the planning process. Some methods focus on large and complicated organizations and have an entire library of books describing a particular approach. You are not expected to use them all. Select the ones that will work for you. There may be parts of these methods that can be incorporated into a small organization.

The following list provides "food for thought" in the different ways to analyze an organization, customer, stakeholder, market, business, etc. I strongly suggest that you track down more detailed instructions in using these tools for analysis. See Appendix D for detailed descriptions.

- **Business Plan:** A basic planning methodology for new and existing organizations in laying out the activities required for success.
- **Statistical Analysis:** Statistics that use past and current performance numbers to speculate on future performance.
- **Technology Planning:** In today's world, almost all organizations require some degree of technology to achieve success and a Technology Plan supports an organization's overall planning effort.
- **SWOT (Strength, Weakness, Opportunity, Threat):** A popular approach to conducting internal and external analysis of an organization's environment.
- **Risk Analysis:** An analysis of current or potential risks that might arise during an organization's activities.
- **Scenario Planning:** An organization imagines realistic paths of action that may be taken by the organization.
- **Prototyping:** An organization conducts a dry run test to determine the probability for success.
- **Balanced Scorecard:** A popular approach to measuring varying aspects of an organization.
- **Benchmarking:** Comparing past performance with current performance to forecast future performance.
- **Forecast Analysis:** An educated and reasonable guess on future activities based upon current trends.
- **Predictive Analytics:** Another tool to predict the future.
- **Vision Plan:** Although not a part of the Strategic Plan, it does not hurt to think beyond reasonable, attainable, and future capabilities.

Ongoing Management Tools:

The following management tools can help manage an organization, identify resources, track trends, and avoid risks. They are discussed in detail in Appendix D.

- **Activity-Based Costing (ABC):** Gathers and tracks cost data which supports planning and decision making. ABC identifies activities, assigns costs to activities, identifies outputs, and then assigns costs to those outputs.

- **Earned Value:** This tool tracks programs by effort, time, and cost. A useful tool to ensure that Goals, Objectives, and Strategies are on track for success.

- **Configuration Management (CM):** CM helps avoid internal issues arising from miscommunications between components.

- **Rolling Analysis:** A methodology for measuring activities over a moving period of time that avoids anomalies. This method also provides earlier awareness of changing trends.

- **Continuity Planning (preparing for disasters):** Part of a risk analysis to identify possible future problems and ways to avoid or reduce the impact.

SUMMARY: Good analysis prepares an organization for the future. It forces an organization to identify and plan for all issues in managing an organization and in producing and delivering the product. As in the case of a Strategic Plan, analysis is an ongoing process, evolving as the organization moves from a startup to an established and expanding organization.

PART EIGHT
HOW STRATEGIC PLANNING DEMYSTIFIED WORKS

The process begins with a look at the horizon to identify what the organization wants to accomplish for the customer (the Mission). Then work its way back, first to identify the major long-term Goals to be accomplished, then to the short-term Objectives that accomplish the Goals, and then to the immediate and specific Strategies you need to start today.

CHART 6

Mission   -   Horizon

Goal   -   Long Term

Objective -   Short Term

Strategy   -   Immediate

Strategic Planning Demystified

Let's begin by outlining the planning process. In summary, here are the chronological actions to be taken.

1. Leadership decides to plan.
2. A designated SPC works with leadership to begin Mission evaluation.
3. SPC trains key personnel on the planning process.
4. Organization conducts customer analysis (looking into the future).
5. Stakeholders' input is obtained.
6. Leadership identifies Mission and Goals (using customer and stakeholder analysis results).
7. SPC and staff identifies key PRMs.
8. Key components identify Objectives and Strategies that support the Mission and Goals.
9. Each Goal, Objective, and Strategy is assigned a manager to be responsible for accomplishing that part of the plan.
10. Organizational structure is validated.
11. Strategic Plan is disseminated and explained to the entire organization.
12. The SPC continues to review and update the plan and PRMs as needed.

DETAILS:

1. **Leadership decides to plan:** The process begins with the organization's leadership (president, CEO, executive person, board of trustees, owner, etc.) deciding that the organization needs a productive and successful Strategic Planning process. Either the organization is new and needs a blueprint for future success or the organization has had a

plan which has become out-of-date or unproductive. Leadership may also feel the need for a new direction or reaffirmation of its current direction.

Leadership will impress upon management the commitment to create a useful and meaningful planning approach. This will be a key moment because managers must buy into the planning process if it is going to be successful.

2. **SPC is designated:** An employee trained in Strategic Planning or a paid consultant becomes the SPC. At this point, the SPC then guides leadership through the process of evaluating the Mission Statement (a desirable and attainable end result for the customer).

3. **SPC trains key personnel on the planning process:** Prior to working on the plan, the organization's leadership, senior management, and line-managers must be instructed on how the planning process works, its structure, and its value. Understanding the planning process will make planning much easier. This is a one-time effort. Once indoctrinated into the process, managers will become better planners.

4. **Organization conducts customer analysis:** The SPC conducts or oversees a customer analysis to determine their current and future requirements. This analysis may require assistance from internal components who have contact with the customers. A review of competitors, industry data, or other relevant sources of information should also be analyzed.

5. **Stakeholders' input is obtained:** For some organizations, there will be a need to confer with some outside organizations. For example, government agencies may need concurrence from the President and/or Congress. Large corporations may need agreement from board of

directors, stockholders, investors, suppliers, distributors, etc. Non-Profit organizations may need to coordinate their planning with both government agencies, foundations, or funding sources. A sole proprietor may need concurrence or support from a spouse. Stakeholder input should be considered and incorporated into the plan.

6. **Leadership identifies Mission and Goals:** The completed customer and Stakeholder Analysis will help leadership formulate or affirm the Mission Statement from which senior management can identify the major Goals that will support the Mission (a continuation of Step 2).

7. **SPC and staff identifies key PRMs:** The Mission and Goals should dictate what PRMs will need to be tracked and what numbers constitute success. If the Mission is to reduce diabetes, then the reduction of diabetes would be the key PRM. If customers want a reliable hybrid vehicle, then the vehicle's reliability record could be a Goal's key PRM.

8. **Key components identify Objectives and Strategies that support the Mission and Goals:** Using the executive Mission and Goals as guidelines, the internal analysis identifies an organization's strengths, weaknesses, risks, and opportunities relating to the customer and stakeholder analysis.

The customer, stakeholder, and internal analyses focuses on what should and can be accomplished for the customer. Results-oriented analysis avoids the pitfall of only focusing on internal Functions or short-term Goals that may be good for the organization but does nothing to help the customer nor the long-term health and success of the organization. The analysis validates the feasibility of the organization's Goals. If issues arise, then management will need to visit the Goals to determine if they should be modified, changed, or dropped.

The managers then share their Objectives and Strategies with other managers so that all components know each other's proposals. In most cases, inconsistencies, weaknesses, etc., will become evident. The senior managers will then coordinate and negotiate with each other to find common ground. This may take several meetings until agreement has been attained.

The SPC wants to attain consensus. If a manager has heartburn over an Objective or Strategy, the SPC needs to sort out the problem. If the manager makes a valid point, an Objective and/or Strategy may need to be modified. The final decision rests with the executive manager who has the final fiduciary responsibility.

The SPC will work with each manager to ensure that they are proposing major organizational Objectives and Strategies that are result-oriented rather than just current Functions. At some later point, the SPC will help each component to identify lower-level Goals, Objectives, Strategies, and Performance Measures that will support the organization's Goals, Objectives, and Strategies. The SPC's job is to ensure that all components' plans support the organization's plan.

9. **Each Goal, Objective, and Strategy is assigned a manager to be responsible for accomplishing that part of the plan:** Next to each Goal, Objective, and Strategy, a manager will be designated with the responsibility for managing and completing that task.

10. **Organizational structure is validated:** Once Goals, Objectives, and Strategies have been selected, any disconnect within the organizational structure should become apparent and can be addressed.

11. **Strategic Plan is disseminated and explained to the entire organization:** At this point, the SPC completes the Strategic Planning document and shares it with leadership and senior managers to ensure everyone is in agreement. Once approved, the document is published. The Strategic Plan is distributed in a three-ring binder so that pages can be updated as necessary. The plan appears at all major meetings. All managers and key personnel have copies, and copies are available to all employees. You can go into any manager's office and find the plan on top of his or her desk with obvious signs that it is being used.

There may be exceptions where sensitive marketing, financial, proprietary, or other sensitive information or activities need to be restricted. In such cases, the information would be removed and replaced with a note indicating that such information was relocated under restricted access.

NOTE: The Strategic Plan can be in an electronic form. A link on the organization's web site or available in a PDF format will allow easier access to the plan and a quicker updating of the plan.

12. **The SPC continues to review and update the plan and PRMs as needed:** Having a plan is not enough. As discussed throughout this book, planning is an ongoing process. As an organization moves forward to accomplish the Mission, Goals, Objectives, and Strategies, reality kicks back. What might have appeared to be easy becomes difficult. What seemed to be inexpensive becomes expensive. If the planning process is to work, it needs to stay in the forefront of the organization. All components must notify the SPC whenever the plan needs to be changed. This is where accountability gets the managers' attention to the plan. If they see a change in the business environment, technology, etc., they need to analyze what impact it will have on the plan and what changes may need to be made.

The SPC also conducts or coordinates the PRMs conducted throughout the organization. The PRMs need to be analyzed to either validate the current plan's direction or to recommend changes or updates to the organization's activities and to the plan.

SUMMARY: The SPC is the key to Strategic Planning implementation. This person vanguards the effort to implement and successfully use the Strategic Planning Demystified approach. An organization can customize its planning approach if it has adequate planning experience. The above suggested implementation process can be changed where needed. Certainly with smaller organizations, some of the above steps can be scaled down or skipped. Whereas, large organization may require additional major activities specific to their requirements.

< >

PART NINE
VISUAL CONCEPT

> The plan should be easy to read.

You could have a great Strategic Plan but if the document itself is wordy and difficult to read, you run the risk of losing the reader. I learned that a well written, visually pleasing planning document is essential for people to understand and use the plan.

Here are a few suggestions when drafting the planning document:

- If you have a paragraph containing a list of items, convert that list into a bullet list. It makes it so much easier to read, comprehend, and retain.

- Generally, sentences should contain no more than three or four prepositional phrases.

- Understand the value of white space in the document. Pages containing long and laborious paragraphs make it difficult to assimilate information. A good example of white space is the "something for dummies" books. They use boxes, bullets, illustrations, charts, etc., to break up and highlight the text into easily understood information.

Lengthy Document: Remember in school when your teacher required a minimum of 500 or 1,000 words in your reports? Teachers believed that without requiring a minimum number of words, students would not put enough effort or information into the composition. This fostered the idea that more is better. As a result, people add a lot of unnecessary words under the assumption that for a document to be authoritative, it has to be long and wordy. As a result, people write long and laborious

Strategic Planning documents rather than letting the information drive the document size. Maybe it's the same reason why people create a plan with an artificial timeline of "five-years." This idea of "more is better" might also explain why organizations insert core value statements that beef up the page count.

Readability - Gunning Fog Index: This index can evaluate a plan's readability and determine what academic level is required to read and comprehend the document. The Gunning Fog Index was developed in 1952 by Robert Gunning. A fog index of 16 requires the reading level of a college graduate (16 years of education). The index helps to determine if the text can be read easily by the intended audience. It looks at the number of syllable words, punctuations, and other elements. Text for a wide audience generally needs a fog index of less than 12. Text requiring near-universal understanding generally needs an index of less than eight. Some word processors have this measurement feature. There are also some free text calculators available on the Internet.

Gobbledygook Language: Say What You Mean. Have you ever read a plan containing cheap clichés, excessive superlatives, bloated adjectives, and hard-to-understand or even incomprehensible phrases? A plan plagued with jargon-laden and overused industrial-strength phrases suggests that the writer doesn't know what is going on and that the document was written in a hollow vacuum with no real down-to-earth substance. A planning document needs to be written in plain language so that everyone understands what needs to be done. Avoiding jargon forces you to be up front and honest in your statements. Hiding behind jargon alerts the readers to possible falsehoods, deceptions, misleading statements, etc.

Does that mean to avoid all jargon? Obviously not. Note the jargon I used in the previous paragraph. Jargon, however, should be limited and should be followed with understandable words making clear what is being said. One way to approach jargon is to read the plan from the customer's point-of-view. Will the customer understand what the organization will accomplish for them when it says, "Conduct phased-in integrated logistical matrix approaches?"

Jargon is used to:

- Make it appear the document is authoritative.
- Hide or confuse the truth (popular with contracting and legal documents).
- Make document appear more intellectual by being long and wordy.
- In limited cases, actually make a good point

Examples of Gobbledygook Phrases:

- Produce greater dynamic return
- Seasoned leaders with deep transformative leadership experience
- Industry-specific experience to help execute discrete projects
- Delivers contemporary re-imagining product lines from regenerated relative resources
- Delivers incremental customer value
- Flexible, scalable, groundbreaking, industry-standard, cutting-edge product from a market-leading, well-positioned, focused, synergized company
- Conducts exploratory research points to millennial third-generation programming
- Delivers exploratory research points to total policy time-phases
- Provides dynamized interactive management consulting services

Strategic Planning Demystified

- Blue-sky approach to deconstructed asset consulting
- Systemized administrative capability
- Revamp and reboot remote modular mobility
- Award-winning boutique management consultancy
- Forward-looking company investing in facilitating digital paradigm shifts
- Holistic and pragmatic approach, rising above the conventional management techniques with its focus on creating agile culture by improving soft skills

Take a moment to allow your head to stop spinning after reading the above examples. Do you know what is meant by: systemized, dynamized, deconstructed asset, re-imagining, discrete projects, digital paradigm shifts, holistic, boutique management, or agile culture? The words sound important and impressive but the fact is, neither you nor I have a clue what they mean. Executives see these words and phrases but are afraid to ask, "What does this mean," in fear of being seen as unhip or out of touch. Instead of demanding that the plan be written in plain language, management quietly signs off on the document, hoping that someone in the organization understands what it means. The document will most likely be filed away, never to be read by anyone.

SUMMARY: The planning document needs to be readable and understandable. I frequently translated technical planning documents into plain English so that executive management could understand the decisions that they needed to make. Trust me, gobbledygook is not a good thing.

< >

Strategic Planning Demystified

PART TEN
ORGANIZATION SIZE

> An organization's size influences the planning methodology.

Large organizations need a detailed and complex Strategic Planning process. For small organizations, however, the planning process does not need to be complex. A small non-profit organization or a small business can clearly see its Mission. For example, a local Lions Club wants to improve economically disadvantaged people's ability to live better lives by providing corrected vision and avoid blindness. The Club knows it can't cure all community eye problems but it can achieve some measurable degree of success. It doesn't need a complicated planning methodology. A Mission, a few Goals, strategies, and Performance Measures are all it needs.

A local restaurant knows that it needs to provide delicious meals in a friendly environment at affordable prices. The auto shop needs to provide good maintenance and repair services. The owner understands and is aware of every aspect of the business. Performance indicators are seen everyday. A small business does not need a complicated Strategic Plan. It needs a list of key actions and activities for the business. Alongside the effort to create a business, the business needs to deliver a product or service that will be desirable by the customer. At the same time, the owner must continue marketing for new customers. New and small organizations only need a short-term plan (six to twelve months). As the business becomes more successful, the owner may need to begin expansion. A long-term plan may now be necessary. The time to think strategically is when the organization begins to thrive and expand.

Strategic Planning Demystified

The topics covered in this book can provide a new or small organization a starting point regarding its Mission and Goals, and how to measure success. As the organization grows, other areas covered in this book can provide assistance to accommodate an expanding planning process.

< >

PART ELEVEN
A FEW LAST WORDS

So the question is this - Has this book given you a better understanding of Strategic Planning? Have you assimilated enough information about Mission, Goals, Objectives, Strategies, and PRMs that will allow you to build a successful Strategic Planning Process? Strategic Planning Demystified is certainly easier to understand than other planning explanations but it does require more real work and analysis to create a useful plan.

- You need to conduct the analysis.

- You need a good understanding of your customer if planning is to be of any value.

- You need a long-term, ongoing planning relationship within your organization, not a one-time planning event.

Planning does require ingenuity and customization. Some planning approaches are not fully successful because organizations shoehorn themselves into a planning approach rather than customizing the planning format to their unique requirements. I believe that all planning methods and approaches, including Strategic Planning Demystified, should adapt to the organization. Use what works.

You should now understand that a true Strategic Planning process is customer driven. As obvious as this appears, so many organizations get tangled in the day-to-day Functions that they begin to forget that the organization exists for its customer. An organization that focuses only on profit is an organization with a higher probability of failure. The only organizations that exist solely for profit would be criminal enterprises (they have victims, not customers).

Strategic Planning Demystified

If an organization's existing planning approach has been highly successful, it might be best not to scrap, replace, or overhaul it for the Strategic Planning Demystified approach. A successful organization, however, may still find parts of the Demystified concept beneficial and in some cases may validate their own method.

Finally, you need a *good planning method that helps your organization successful move into the future.* I believe that this book contains an approach that will help you attain that success.

< >

APPENDIX A
MISSION STATEMENT EXAMPLES

The following examples provide further opportunity to discuss and analyze Mission Statements. After each Mission Statement, I've provided a short analysis explaining how I would approach, formulate, and create the Mission Statement. I've used a variety of examples. My intention is to help you craft a statement that is effective and meaningful. You can search the Internet for Mission Statement examples and conduct your own analysis. Practice will make you better at creating a good Mission Statement. As you read these examples, consider what the supporting Goals and PRMs should be.

I've highlighted in bold and italic print what I consider the core Mission Statement (customer benefit). I've grouped the statements under business, non-profit, and government titles.

NOTE: Regarding business and non-profit examples, I have not identified the organization because it is not relevant. In some cases, I've altered the Mission Statements to demonstrate good, acceptable, and weaker statements. I have identified the Federal agencies but in some cases I've altered their statements for demonstration purposes. The reader is responsible for his or her choices, actions, and/or results in using the suggestions contained herein. Please do not cite these examples as accurate reflections of an organization's Mission. Search the Internet to find an organization's current and official Mission Statement.

GROUP 1 - GOOD MISSION STATEMENTS

BUSINESS EXAMPLES:

Retailer: *Provide customer-valued solutions* with the best prices, products, and services to make the company the first choice for home improvement.

> **Analysis:** Great statement. Can be measured for performance. This statement could be used for almost any home improvement retailer. What do you think would be the Goals for this retailer?

Restaurant: *Delight customers* with high-quality, delicious products while balancing the needs of our employees, guests, and stockholders.

> **Analysis:** Excellent statement. "Delight customers" goes to the core Mission of all restaurants and represents the Performance Measurement. This restaurant will accomplish the Mission by providing "high-quality, delicious products." There is a second Mission regarding the needs of employees, guests, and stockholders. I'm not sure if it's needed and might be best handled as a Goal(s). It also raises the question, is a guest the same as a customer?

Entertainment Company: *Make people happy.*

> **Analysis:** A great Mission Statement. Having visited its facility, I know first hand the great effort that this organization and staff take to make people happy. The statement is easily remembered and understood by its staff. The Mission is accomplished throughout its facility, including the bathrooms.

Medical Company:

- *Help diagnose, alleviate, and/or cure diseases.*

- *Improve the quality and adequacy of the global food supply.*
- *Contribute significantly to an active, modern lifestyle.*
- *Protect the climate and address the consequences of climate change.*

Analysis: Excellent Mission Statements. The company clearly sees four distinct Missions which can be measured for success. The fourth statement seems out of place but in a social context, it might be appropriate from a public relations angle. What kind of Goals do you think would support each Mission?

Retail Company: *Meet the needs of its customers* for total value by offering a unique package of location, price, service, and product.

Analysis: Meeting the customer's needs is the core Mission for any retailer regardless of the commodity. The end of the statement tells how it will accomplish the Mission. Both customers and employees can clearly understand the Mission. The last part could represent the Goals.

Retail Store: We save people money so *they can live better.*

Analysis: Short, sweet, and to the point. The Mission drives to keep prices as low as possible and provide products and services that help customers to live better. Now, it is possible to reverse the phrases to "help people live better by helping them save money" but because the statement is short, the original statement is fine.

Technology Company: Promote openness, innovation & opportunity on the Web.

Analysis: A great Mission. The word "Web" is another word for "customer." Easily remembered and clearly measurable.

Small Business Mission Statement Examples:

- **Photographers:** Make memories to be cherished for generations. Preserve family memories through photographic artistry
- **Restaurant:** Serve delicious and affordable meals in a calm and delightful setting.
- **Fast Food Restaurant:** Deliver fast, affordable, and delicious meals.
- **Small Health Food Restaurant:** Deliver fast, affordable, delicious, and healthy meals.
- **Small Health Food Store:** Provide healthy and nutritious foods at affordable prices.
- **Auto Repair:** Repair cars that stay repaired the first time.
- **Auto Repair:** Service vehicles correctly in a timely manner and at an affordable price.

Analysis: A small business Mission Statement should be easy because the business delivers a specific product or service that the customer wants or needs. As previously mentioned, companies that provide similar services have similar Missions. But a small business can focus on one or two elements that will be important to its specific clientele.

It should also be pointed out that for small and new businesses, the Mission needs to be achievable within a short period of time. In fact, the business should strive to achieve the Mission on the first day and maintain that level of service into the future. As the business grows, the Mission may grow or change. For example, the small auto repair shop may decide to expand, so the Mission might add, "serve more customers by expanding to other parts of the community" or "increase customer accessibility by expanding service centers throughout the metropolitan area" with a new Goal to expand or franchise the business.

NON-PROFIT EXAMPLES:

Eye Institute: *Restore vision and prevent blindness.*

Goals:

- *Find new treatments* through research.
- *Improve medical skills* through education.
- *Rehabilitate* those who have lost vision.
- *Identify and treat eye disease* through community outreach program.

Analysis: The Mission is absolutely clear and understandable: restore and prevent blindness. You can easily create measurements for restoring and preventing. I've included the Goals to demonstrate that having a good Mission Statement creates Goals focused on the Mission. Can you list the Objectives that would support the Goals?

Medical Association: *Cure cancer* through cancer research.

Analysis: Excellent Mission Statement with a high risk of failure. In fact, it's almost too bold a statement unless there is sufficient evidence that a cure is achievable.

Medical Association: *Build healthier lives, free of cardiovascular diseases and strokes.*

Analysis: Another excellent and clearly stated statement. The word "free" may be a risky Mission but it certainly will drive the organization to work hard. Maybe the word "reduce" would be better and more attainable.

Health Association: *Keep people healthy* through disease management services that help patients avoid the hospital.

> **Analysis:** Though it has a high risk of failure, it certainly keeps its staff focused on the basic reason they exist: keep customers healthy. I would rephrase the statement to say, "***Keep people healthy to avoid the hospital. . . .***" What Goals would support this Mission?

Fund Raising Organization: Doing whatever it takes to *save a child.*

> **Analysis:** An excellent broad statement that simply says that a child at risk is its business. Goals should focus on programs that can be measured by the number of children saved. I might suggest rewriting the statement to say, "Save children by doing whatever it takes." The "whatever it takes" could be replaced with more specific actions or Goals (e.g., expanding social services, increasing intervention, raising financial resources).

Fund Raising Organization: *Improve lives* by mobilizing the caring power of communities to advance the common good.

> **Analysis:** If you belong to or contribute to this organization, you can easily remember "improve lives" and use those two words to measure success.

University: *Prepare students for productive and meaningful lives* through education and enlightenment.

> **Analysis:** Good Mission Statement. Success can be measured by the students' success in attaining their vocation. The word "prepare" is

almost a Function word. To be bolder, the statement could say, "Help students attain productive and meaningful lives . . ."

University Department of Safety & Security: *Ensure a safe and secure environment* that facilitates an extraordinary learning experience for all members of the campus community.

> **Analysis:** Excellent statement. This Mission Statement demonstrates a good example of an administrative, indirect component that recognizes that it supports the organization's main Mission by providing a safe environment for learning.

Social Movement Organization: *Equality for everyone* for political, educational, social, and economic rights by eliminating race-based discrimination practices.

> **Analysis:** Excellent Mission Statement. Having the heart of the Mission at the beginning, "equality for everyone," should keep the organization focused on what is most important.

GOVERNMENT EXAMPLES:

Security Division:

- *Ensure a safe and secure work environment* for employees and others with access to facilities.
- *Prevent the compromise of national security and information.*

> **Analysis:** A strong and excellent statement. They recognize what is important and what must be done. Failure represents a significant negative impact to its customers (the agency and the US). I don't think you can improve on this Mission Statement.

Food and Drug Administration:

- *Protecting the public health* by assuring the safety, efficacy, and security of human and veterinary drugs, biological products, medical devices, our nation's food supply, cosmetics, and products that emit radiation.

- *Advancing the public health* by helping to speed innovations that make medicines and foods more effective, safer, and more affordable.

- *Improving the public health* by providing accurate, science-based information they need when using medicines and foods.

   Analysis: Excellent Mission Statements. The Missions are clear and measurable. The Missions contain the performance words of protecting, advancing, and improving. The descriptors (e.g., safety of drugs, innovations, and accurate information) could represent the Goals to be accomplished for the Mission.

U.S. Coast Guard:

- *Save those in peril.*
- *Protect the maritime economy and the environment.*
- *Defend our maritime borders.*

   Analysis: Contains three excellent Mission Statements. Easily remembered and easily measured for success. I would consider "*Save those in peril*" as the strongest statement.

Environmental Protection Agency (EPA): *Protect human health and the environment.*

   Analysis: Short and to the point. What Goals (actions) do you think would support the protection of health and environment? At an agency level, the Goals will probably be broad and long-term.

U.S. State Department: *Create a more secure, democratic, and prosperous world* for the benefit of the American people and the international community.

> **Analysis:** The statement could almost be a vision statement except for the inclusion of the word "more" which is the performance indicator to improve. The Goals can define the specific effort required although I suspect the Goals will be broad and long term.

U.S. Department of Homeland Security:

- Lead the unified national effort to *secure America.*
- *Prevent and deter terrorist attacks.*
- *Protect against and respond to threats and hazards* to the nation.
- *Secure our national borders* while welcoming lawful immigrants, visitors, and trade.

> **Analysis:** Good Mission Statements which can be measured. They have a high potential for failure; which is good because it means that success will have a significant positive impact. The Mission "*secure America*" could be the Mission Statement. The other three Missions could be Goals which would be supported by the Missions of the various agencies within Homeland Security: Coast Guard, Immigration, Secret Service, Customs, Transportation Security, etc. Search these components to see how or if they support the Homeland Security Missions.

SUMMARY: The above examples contain clear and distinct action words, such as, prevent, protect, improve, prepare, strengthen, etc. These words can be measured for success or failure. Multiple Mission Statements generally represent different products and/or services to the same or different customers.

GROUP 2 - ACCEPTABLE EXAMPLES

These examples are alright but need some modification by moving the Mission Statement to the beginning or reword the core statement to become more measurable.

BUSINESS EXAMPLES:

Computer Company: Organize the world's information and *make it universally accessible and useful.*

> **Analysis:** Although the statement appears to be almost a Vision Statement, I think that this organization could focus its services on a global scale. As with other statements, I would put the core Mission at the beginning. The word "organize" could be seen as a Function which would generate Function Goals rather than Performance Goals. The real Mission should be, "Make information accessible and useful."

Consulting Company: *Provide professional, reliable, and long-term solutions today, at yesterday's prices.*

> **Analysis:** A good statement but I'm concerned about the "at yesterday's prices" because yesterday's prices may be higher than today's prices. I would rather see a performance adjective in the beginning, such as, "Provide *better* professional, reliable, and long-term solutions at affordable and reasonable prices."

Aircraft Company: To *push the leading edge of aviation*, taking huge challenges *doing what others cannot do.*

Analysis: A good, bold statement. I'm not sure about the phrase "taking huge challenges." Sounds like the company always takes on large risks.

Computer Company: *Change the way businesses manage email* by eliminating their need to purchase and deploy costly email-related software, hardware, and security services.

Analysis: Good statement. I would suggest modifying "change the way" to "improve the way" because change isn't always a good thing.

Manufacturer: *To solve unsolved problems innovatively.*

Analysis: Obviously the company's core Mission is to solve problems. I'm concerned with the word "innovatively." Must all solutions be innovative? Will the company reinvent the wheel every time to solve a client's problem? Will all the Goals focus on innovation? I would suggest dropping the word innovatively unless, in fact, that is the only way the company solves problems.

Computer Company: *Solve complex network computing problems* for governments, enterprises, and service providers.

Analysis: I like the "solve complex problems" statement but do they only work on problems? Do they offer customers services that improve existing systems? After they solve problems, do they go away or continue to ensure problems don't reoccur?

Retail Company:
- To make, distribute, and sell *the finest quality all natural ice cream and euphoric concoctions* with a continued commitment to incorporating wholesome, natural ingredients.

- *Promoting business practices that respect the Earth and the Environment.*

    Analysis: The first few words are Functions (make, distribute, and sell). I would suggest beginning with "Give the customer the finest quality. . ." Making and distributing are important internal Goals in support of delivering quality products to the customer.

    The second Mission appears to be more of a marketing tool. Will the customer buy a product because the company respects the Earth? I suspect this statement is to separate the company from the perception that most companies are bad for the environment. And where does the customer fit into the second Mission?

Computer Company: Committed to *bringing the best personal computing experience* to students, educators, creative professionals, and consumers around the world through its innovative hardware, software and Internet offerings.

    Analysis: Good statement. I almost moved this to the excellent category except I would have preferred a more dynamic beginning, such as "Bring (or Deliver) the best . . ." Being "committed to" does not necessarily require you to accomplish it. It is almost a Function word.

Computer Company: *Help people and businesses* throughout the world *realize their full potential.*

    Analysis: Good but not great. Almost too broad. I'm not sure what "realize their full potential" really means or how to measure it. The word "help" is adequate but can be more of a Function. How would you reword this Mission Statement?

Automobile Manufacturer:

- Multinational corporation *engaged in socially responsible operations* worldwide.

- Provide products and services of such quality that *our customers will receive superior value.*

- Employees and business partners will *share in our success.*

- Stock-holders will receive a *sustained superior return on their investment.*

   Analysis: We have four Missions. The second one is the most important, "Customers will receive superior value." The third and fourth are secondary and dependent on the success of the second statement. The first statement is a Core Value Statement. It raises the question, why must it be stated as a Mission?

Restaurant:

- Provide quick food service to *fulfill our guest's needs* more accurately, quickly, courteously, and *in a cleaner environment* than our competitors.

- *Conduct all our business affairs ethically*, and with the best employees.

- *Grow profitably and responsibly.*

- Provide *career advancement opportunities* for every willing member of our organization.

   Analysis: The first statement is the real Mission. It could be modified by moving "fulfill our guest's needs" to the front. I'm not sure about the other statements and whether they should be Goals. When an organization inserts a core value (the second statement), it begs the question, why? Has this restaurant been caught being unethical? Good ethics is a Function that all organizations strive to achieve or maintain. It should only be put into the Mission if events have caused customers to question the organization's ethics (which in itself is not a good sign).

Credit Union: To create quality financial relationships for a lifetime by providing valuable financial products and services that *exceed members' expectations.*

> **Analysis:** Good statement. Move the core statement to the beginning and say, "Exceed member's financial expectations by providing quality financial products and services."

Bank: We want to be the *best financial services company* in the world.

> **Analysis:** Good statement. Striving to be the best in the world might be reaching too far but if the bank has a good plan to reach out around the globe, then it's a good statement. The phrase "We want to be" sounds like a Vision rather than a Mission. I would suggest something like "provide" or "deliver" the best financial services.

Auto repair shop: Be the *most professional repair and service shop* in the market by the value we create and the relationships we build with our customers and employees.

> **Analysis:** I like this statement, but I would like to see "customers" stated earlier in the statement. For example, "Provide customers the most professional and best value repair and service shop." Surveying the customers will indicate if the company is meeting the Mission.

Bank: *To make the world a better place to live by*:

- Helping our **Clients achieve economic success and financial security.**
- Creating a place where our employees can **learn, grow, and be fulfilled in their work.**
- Making the communities in which we work **better places to be.**

> **Analysis:** The first line is a bit broad but the first and third bullets clarify it. The second bullet is an Objective that would help support a higher Goal. I would prefer a Mission Statement that simply says, "Help clients achieve economic and financial success." The bullets would then represent Goals.

NON-PROFIT EXAMPLES:

University: Provide quality graduate and undergraduate academic programs. The University seeks to educate a diverse student population, *providing these students with the knowledge and skills necessary to attain both academic and career Goals.*

> **Analysis:** The Mission Statement is buried at the end of the statement. I would prefer a stronger statement in the beginning, such as, "Students attain their career Goals by providing them . . ." Helping the students (customers) attain their vocation (Mission) is more important than providing quality academic programs (Functions). Focusing on the student's requirements should result in providing quality programs to meet those requirements.

College: *Strengthen communities* by giving everyone the opportunity to learn and develop the right skills.

> **Analysis:** I'm not sure about the word "everyone" but the statement does start with a measurable Mission although the word "communities" is a bit vague. How would you rewrite this statement?

Fund Raising Organization: Promote and support philanthropy through a program that is employee-focused, cost-efficient, and effective in providing all employees the opportunity to ***improve the quality of life for all.***

> **Analysis:** The statement, "Promote and support philanthropy" are Functions. I would be concerned that the organization would focus on "promote and support" (Functions) rather than improve the quality of life (Mission). Need to move that last part to the beginning. The "for all" statement might be too broad. What does "employee-focused" mean and why?

GOVERNMENT EXAMPLES:

Federal Emergency Management Agency: Support our citizens and first responders to ensure that as a nation we work together to build, sustain, and improve our capability to ***prepare for, protect against, respond to, recover from, and mitigate all hazards.***

> **Analysis:** I would move the core statement to the beginning. In fact, there are a multitude of Missions in this statement. The current Mission is to "support." I would rewrite to say, "Improve the nation's ability to protect against, respond to, recover from, and avoid all known and potential hazards and disasters."

National Weather Service (NWS): Provides weather, hydrologic, and climate forecasts and warnings for the United States, its territories, adjacent waters and ocean areas, for the ***protection of life and property and the enhancement of the national economy.*** NWS data and products form a national information database and infrastructure which can be used by other governmental agencies, the private sector, the public, and the global community.

> **Analysis:** The core Mission Statement is buried in the middle, surrounded by Function Statements. Need to move the Mission to the beginning and rewrite and shorten the Function Statements. A short Mission Statement would be, "Protect life and property, and enhance the national economy through improved weather, hydrologic, and climate forecasts and warnings."

U.S. Navy: Maintain, train, and equip combat-ready Naval forces capable of *winning wars, deterring aggression and maintaining freedom of the seas.*

> **Analysis:** The core Mission at the end needs to be moved to the beginning and reworded with stronger and aggressive words, "Win wars, deter aggression, and maintain freedom of the seas by . . ." Again, let's put the Mission at the beginning. The Mission is not to maintain, train, and equip. They are Functions that could be Goals.

N. Carolina Dept. of State: *To serve and protect* citizens, the business community and governmental agencies by facilitating business activities, by providing accurate and timely information, and by preserving documents and records.

> **Analysis:** Nice statement but too broad. "*To serve and protect*" from what? Sounds like a law enforcement Mission. The phrases at the end of the statement could be Goals.

Small Business Development Center: To advise, train, and inform small businesses to *help them achieve success.*

Analysis: Mission should be "Help small businesses achieve success." The "advising, training, and informing" would make good Goals.

SUMMARY: Most of the above examples contain a Mission Statement buried in the middle or end of the statement. Some start with a list of Function Statements which could lead to a set of Function Goals.

GROUP 3 - WEAKER STATEMENTS

BUSINESS EXAMPLES:

Computer Company: Engage collaboratively with our clients and *tackle their most complex business problems.*

> **Analysis:** Is the company only a problem solver? Seems to be a narrow Mission Statement. What does it mean to "engage collaboratively with our clients?" Do they only handle the most complex problems?

Beverage Company:
- To *refresh* the world
- To *inspire* moments of optimism and happiness
- To *create value and make a difference*

> **Analysis:** Sounds more like jingles than Mission Statements. The last bullet is the closest to a Mission Statement but is still vague. Make a difference to what?

Retailer:
- Dedicated to *bringing new and creative ideas* to the market place, both in our product offerings as well as our marketing events.

- We will continue to ***develop our unique brand positioning, to maintain and grow*** our solid brand recognition, and to adhere to ***high quality*** design standards.

- Because everyone wants to have fun everyday, company will continue to ***offer something for everyone with fun always in mind***

   Analysis: The imbedded Mission Statements are good but should be at the beginning of each bullet. The second Mission sounds more like a set of Goals. The last Mission is the closest to a good Mission, "offer something for everyone."

Investment Company: ***Provide one-stop progressive economic development services*** through partnerships on behalf of shareholders and the community.

   Analysis: What is the result (Mission) to be achieved by providing "services?" What word or words do you think need to be added? Are the shareholders and community the customers?

Bank: Our product: ***Service***. Our value-added: ***Financial Advice***. Our competitive advantage: ***Our People***.

   Analysis: Nice statements but not challenging. They beg the questions, what kind of service, what kind of advice, and what kind of people? And of course, we see that buzz phrase "value-added." All banks try to give good financial advice. Instead of "value-added," say good or profitable advice. As a customer, what do you want from your bank?

Corporation: Provide online scientific and educational material and support to the scientific community and general public, relating to aerospace, renewable energy, and other scientific disciplines. Fosters learning and academic excellence by working with scientists, educators, and inventors to create a safe, fulfilling, and academically enriching environment for **breakthrough science.**

> **Analysis:** A long list of Functions. The last phrase, "breakthrough science" might be the Mission. The statement does describe its customer base but needs a better description of the corporate services in order to stand out from other corporations. I would word the Mission as "**Create breakthrough science by . . .**"

Law Firm: The cornerstones upon which our civil legal system is built, justice, equality, and fairness, are what our legal firm stands for. Integrity, honesty, and compassion are the pillars upon which our firm stands, which we bring to our practice every day. The attorneys and staff of our law firm are **dedicated advocates of our clients, protecting their rights and providing them a voice in the courtroom.** (Followed by five long sentences.) Simply, we are **committed to fighting for our clients** in dignified, professional and honest manner. We will not stop until justice has been served.

> **Analysis:** I'll bet that no one in this law office can repeat their Mission Statement. Most of this is fluff. I removed five sentences from the middle and it's still too long. What is most important from the client's point-of-view? How about a straight forward statement, "We fight to win for our clients in and out of the court room."

Grocery Store: To be a **leader in the distribution and merchandising** of food, pharmacy, health and personal care items, seasonal merchandise, and related products and services

> **Analysis:** I see a risk of focusing on Functions (distribution and merchandising) instead of the customer. Can this grocery store be

the leader in distribution and merchandising while failing customer requirements? Will employees focus on distribution and merchandising and miss the mark with customers? The store believes that if it can deliver merchandise, that the customers will buy.

NON-PROFIT EXAMPLES:

University: The discovery and dissemination of new knowledge are central to its Mission. Through its focus on teaching and learning, research and discovery, and outreach and engagement, the university creates, conveys, and applies knowledge to *expand personal growth and opportunity, advance social and community development, foster economic competitiveness, and improve the quality of life.*

> **Analysis:** There appears to be multiple Missions. The first sentence suggests that research (discovery and dissemination) is the prime Mission. The second, long sentence contains Functions and ends with a list of Missions. I'm not sure where the students (customers) are represented in this Mission Statement.

University: To *educate.* (Followed by eight paragraphs.)

> **Analysis:** This is a Function Statement which is safe and easy to accomplish. An institution can educate but that doesn't mean students will achieve their vocation. The eight paragraphs are so wordy that no one is ever going to remember any of it.

NOTE: One of the great mysteries is why institutions of higher learning have some of the worst Mission Statements. That is why I have inserted several school examples.

University Undergraduate Program: Expects that the scholarship and collegiality it fosters in its students will ***lead them in their later lives to advance knowledge, to promote understanding, and to serve society.*** (Last sentence in a very long paragraph.)

> **Analysis:** Again, a long paragraph with just a hint of a Mission at the end of the Mission Statement. It would be interesting to know if the university follows up on students to determine if the students' university education contributed to their careers.

Magnet School: Create a better world through education.

- Develop inquiring, knowledgeable and caring young people who help to **create a better and more peaceful world** through intercultural understanding and respect.

- Works with schools, governments and international organizations to ***develop challenging programs*** of international education and rigorous assessment.

- Encourage students across the world to become **active, compassionate and lifelong learners** who understand that other people, with their differences, can also be right.

> **Analysis:** The Mission Statement seems to be more of a vision statement followed by three bullets. The first bullet appears to be a Vision Statement. The second bullet could be a Goal. The third might be the Mission. This is a magnet school, not the United Nations. They need to come off the cloud and describe the end-results for their students (customers).

University: Offers a diverse array of innovative academic programs at the undergraduate, graduate, and professional levels, complementing on-campus educational opportunities and resources with accessible distance learning programs, and fostering intellectual inquiry, leadership, and commitment to community through engagement of students and faculty in *a dynamic, life-long learning environment.*

> **Analysis:** A long Function Statement with a hint of a Mission at the end. Is the "*life-long learning environment*" for the students (customers) or the University?

University:

- Combines a tradition of strong undergraduate and graduate education with a focus on *community and public service*.

- We integrate teaching, research, and creative activity in an engaging, challenging, and supportive learning environment to *prepare productive citizens for our state and the world.*

> **Analysis:** The first statement suggests that the education is targeting community and public service which seems a bit narrow. The second statement ends with a decent Mission Statement, if the word "citizens" refers to the students (customer).

University: As one of the nation's distinguished comprehensive universities, the resources of the university constitute *an invaluable asset* for the intellectual, economic, and social enrichment, while the international prestige of the university *enhances the image of the state* throughout the world.

> **Analysis:** Should the Mission be the enhancement of the state's image? The University appears to be more concerned about its image than in its students' (customers') success.

Health Organization: An international network of people who are concerned about health-related frauds, myths, fads, fallacies, and misconduct. Its primary focus is on ***quackery-related information*** that is difficult or impossible to get elsewhere.

> **Analysis:** This statement contains only Functions. Being concerned or providing information is an easy Function. "***Preventing people from falling victim to medical fraud***" should be the Mission.

Social Organization:

- Provide information for concerned Americans about critical national security issues.

- Influence public policy by encouraging dialogue between American citizens and their elected representatives in order to produce legislation and executive action that ***enhances the national security*** of the United States.

> **Analysis:** The first statement is a Function Statement. Answering the question of "why provide information" will identify the true Mission. The second statement falls short of being a Mission Statement because the policy is vague. "***Enhancing the national security***" would make a good Mission Statement if followed by Goals that would improve security.

Organization: A resource by and for women gamers dedicated to ***increasing the voices of underrepresented identities*** in the game development industries and in gamer communities.

> **Analysis:** I think I see a Mission Statement but I'm not sure what it is. Maybe the Mission is to "***Improve women's influence and contribution to the world of games***."

Organization: To *inspire personal connections* to the natural world and responsible actions to sustain it.

> **Analysis:** Reads more like a Vision Statement. How do you measure "inspiration?" Who is the customer?

GOVERNMENT EXAMPLES:

Office of Native American Affairs: Ensure that American Indians, Native Alaskans, and Native Hawaiians seeking to create, develop and expand small businesses *have full access* to the necessary business development and expansion tools available through the Agency's entrepreneurial development, lending and procurement programs.

> **Analysis:** The Mission is implied but weak because it only wants to ensure access to business tools. That is a Function. It could be stronger by declaring that its Mission is to "*help American Indians, et. al., achieve business success in creating, developing, and expanding their small businesses.*" This agency appears to be a library of information. Success by Native people in building or sustaining new businesses would not be a PRM under the current Mission but rather how many times the services are accessed, which is an output, not an outcome measurement.

United States Coast Guard Academy: Committed to *strengthening the nation's future* by educating, developing, training, and inspiring leaders of character who are ethically, intellectually, professionally, and physically *prepared to serve their country and humanity*, and who are strong in their *resolve to build* on the long military and maritime heritage and proud accomplishments of the United States Coast Guard.

> **Analysis:** By now, you should be able to spot the problems with this Mission Statement. The first part is too broad and contains mostly

Functions (e.g., educating, developing, training). "Prepared to serve their country and humanity," is better but still vague. The third Mission to "resolve to build" is really vague. How does this Mission connect with the Coast Guard's Mission to save those in peril, protect the maritime economy and the environment, and defend our maritime borders? Shouldn't the Academy's Mission be a Goal to support the Coast Guard's Mission to save lives by creating the best trained officers who are trained in leadership, management, etc.?

National Cancer Institute (NCI): The National Cancer Institute *coordinates* the National Cancer Program, which conducts and supports research, training, health information dissemination, and other programs with respect to the cause, diagnosis, prevention, and treatment of cancer, rehabilitation from cancer, and the continuing care of cancer patients and the families of cancer patients. Specifically, the Institute:

- *Supports and coordinates* research projects conducted by universities, hospitals, research foundations, and businesses throughout this country and abroad through research grants and cooperative agreements.
- *Conducts research* in its own laboratories and clinics.
- *Supports* education and training in fundamental sciences and clinical disciplines for participation in basic and clinical research programs and treatment programs relating to cancer through career awards, training grants, and fellowships.
- *Supports* research projects in cancer control.
- *Supports* a national network of cancer centers.
- *Collaborates* with voluntary organizations and other national and foreign institutions engaged in cancer research and training activities.

- *Encourages and coordinates cancer research* by industrial concerns where such concerns evidence a particular capability for programmatic research.
- *Collects and disseminates information* on cancer.
- *Supports construction* of laboratories, clinics, and related facilities necessary for cancer research through the award of construction grants.

Analysis: I've included this statement because it's obvious what is wrong. Too long, too wordy, too much. It "conducts" and "supports" (Functions) a lot of activities. A very safe approach. NCI doesn't see itself as doing anything but Functions. I'll bet that it measures success by the number of research projects created or managed, not the progress in defeating cancer. Remember, Functions measure Functions, not Results. How would you rewrite NCI's Mission in ten words or less?

Federal Reserve System: *Provide the nation with a safer, more flexible, and more stable monetary and financial system.* Over the years, its role in banking and the economy has expanded.

Today, the Federal Reserve's duties fall into four general areas:

- Conducting the nation's monetary policy by *influencing* the monetary and credit conditions in the economy in pursuit of maximum employment, stable prices, and moderate long-term interest rates.
- Supervising and regulating banking institutions to *ensure the safety and soundness* of the nation's banking and financial system and *to protect* the credit rights of consumers.
- *Maintaining the stability* of the financial system and containing systemic risk that may arise in financial markets.

- ***Providing financial services*** to depository institutions, the U.S. government, and foreign official institutions, including playing a major role in operating the nation's payments system.

    Analysis: The initial statement is good. The list contained within the Mission Statement, however, should be the Goals or rewritten as mini-Missions.

Federal Documents Section, State Library: *Select and help disseminate* Federal government documents, information, and related materials to supplement the general collection of the State Library.

   Analysis: The Mission appears to be Function in nature. It might help to add "relevant" or "important" or "useful" or some criteria that the Library uses in selecting documents. What is the purpose to "supplement the general collection?" I would think a better Mission would be to "*improve the public's understanding of government activities by providing selective but pertinent documents on Federal activities relating to the state.*"

Defense Industrial Security Clearance Office-DISCO Mission:

- ***Determining*** the personnel clearance eligibility of employees for access to classified information, foreign or domestic.

- ***Maintenance*** of personnel clearance records and furnishing information to authorized activities.

- ***Processing*** security assurances, clearances and visits involving the United States and foreign countries.

- ***Monitoring*** the contractor's continued eligibility in the National Industrial Security Program.

Analysis: Again, you should be able to recognize a Mission Statement full of Function Statements. Who is the customer to be served by DISCO? By listing only Functions to determine, maintain, process, and monitor a person's eligibility, DISCO avoids accepting responsibility for the results. I would suggest a strong statement to "*protect and keep American military and industrial information safe by ensuring only trusted individuals have access to sensitive information.*" Isn't hiring trusted individuals the Mission?

Department of Agriculture (DOA): *Provide leadership* on food, agriculture, natural resources, rural development, nutrition, and related issues based on sound public policy, the best available science, and efficient management.

Analysis: The Mission is weak because "leadership" sounds like a Function. What result is this agency attempting to achieve for Americans, and how do we measure success? Shouldn't the DOA be working towards safe food, good nutrition, natural resources, etc.?

Defense Advanced Research Projects Agency: *Creating breakthrough technologies* for national security.

Analysis: The Mission is followed by three long paragraphs which might clarify the need for breakthrough technologies. But a review fails disclose what is to be achieved for the American people (customers).

Drug Enforcement Administration (DEA): Enforce the controlled substances laws and regulations of the United States and bring to the criminal and civil justice system of the United States, or any other competent jurisdiction, those organizations and principal members of organizations, involved in the growing, manufacture, or distribution of controlled substances appearing in or destined for illicit traffic in the

United States; and to recommend and support non-enforcement programs aimed at reducing the availability of illicit controlled substances on the domestic and international markets.

> **Analysis:** Contains a long list of Functions. Being a law enforcement agency, it would seem that its Mission is to make America safer. DEA's Mission sounds like the wording that would be contained in the DEA's statutory language. I suspect that closer inspection to the statutory authority will say something about making America safer by removing illegal controlled substances.

SUMMARY: As the above examples demonstrate, it is important to identify exactly what your Mission will be and place it at the beginning of your statement to ensure everyone understands where you are going. I would suggest searching the Internet for the phrase "Mission Statement" and critiquing the Mission Statements you find. And while you're at it, ask yourself, what kind of Goals would be needed to accomplish the Mission?

< >

APPENDIX B
VISION VERSUS MISSION

As mentioned earlier in the book, Vision is not part of planning because of several reasons, including the confusion between how Mission and Vision Statements are defined. Let's look at examples for different organizations. You will observe that some Mission Statements appear to be similar to the Vision Statements. These comparisons demonstrate why writing and including a Vision Statement in the Strategic Plan might result in a poor, weak, or Function-type Mission Statement, followed by weaker Goals and Objectives.

Medical Association:

Vision: A world without Alzheimer's disease.

Mission:

- Eliminate Alzheimer's disease through the advancement of research.
- Provide and enhance care and support for all affected.
- Reduce the risk of dementia through the promotion of brain health

Analysis: Good Vision Statement. The first Mission, however, is also focused on eliminating Alzheimer's disease. So, eliminate the Vision Statement and let the Mission Statement be "eliminate Alzheimer's disease," providing that the organization has a real plan that will eliminate Alzheimer's disease. How does the second and third Missions support the Vision? Do you see the disconnect between the Vision and these Missions?

Retailer:

Vision: Be the world's beer company. Through all of our products, services and relationships, we will add to life's enjoyment.

Mission: To brew, package, and ship the freshest, highest quality beer in the world in the most efficient and responsible manner possible.

> **Analysis:** This example shows where the Vision is a Mission and the Mission is a set of Functions which will lead to weak or Function Goals (brew, package and ship). Although being the world's beer to add to life's enjoyment will be difficult to achieve, if the company has a plan to attain number one beer status, then the Vision Statement should be the Mission Statement.
>
> The Mission Statement starts with Functions in support of a Performance Measure (quality) and then returns back to Functions. The current Mission Statement consists of possible Goals or Objectives. I would suggest a Mission of "giving customers a great (or best) satisfying beer drinking experience."

Cosmetic Company:

Vision: Best understands and satisfies the product, service and self-fulfillment needs of women - globally.

Mission: Build a unique portfolio of beauty and related brands, striving to surpass competitors in quality, innovation and value, and elevating our image to become the beauty company most women turn to worldwide. (followed by multiple Mission Statements)

> **Analysis:** The Vision Statement is clearly a Mission Statement. The Mission Statement contains a subtle Mission surrounded by

Goals. This will result in Goals that will focus on Functions and will lead to measuring Functions and not results.

Manufacturer:

Vision: Be the global leader in customer value.

Mission: Company will be the leader in providing the best value in products and support services for customers dedicated to building the world's infrastructure and developing and transporting its resources. We provide the best value to customers. (Followed by three other Mission Statements.)

Analysis: Both the Vision and Mission refers to wanting to be the "leader" and have "customer value" suggesting that the Mission and Vision Statements are saying the same thing. I would combine both into one Mission Statement.

Defense Industrial Security Clearance Office (DISCO):

Vision: Be the focal point of interaction and premier provider of industrial security and education services for the U.S. Government and the companies in the National Industrial Security Program in support of national security.

Mission:

- Determining the personnel clearance eligibility of employees for access to classified information, foreign or domestic.

- Maintenance of personnel clearance records and furnishing information to authorized activities.

- Processing security assurances, clearances, and visits involving the United States and foreign countries.

- Monitoring the contractor's continued eligibility in the National Industrial Security Program.

Analysis: The Vision and the Mission describe Functions. The Vision describes activities that it should be accomplishing now, not in the future (Vision). The Mission should be to "protect and keep American military and industrial information safe by ensuring that only trustworthy individuals have access to sensitive information." A strong Mission Statement can keep the agency focused on improving and maintaining a strong background check process. But as written, DISCO will most likely measure success by tabulating clearance eligibility, information furnished, things processed, and contracts monitored. Can you see the disconnect here? DISCO is focused on Functions, not results.

Chemical Company:

Vision: To be the world's most dynamic science company, creating sustainable solutions essential to a better, safer, and healthier life for people everywhere.

Mission:

- Maintaining sustainable growth.
- Increasing shareholder and societal value while reducing our environmental footprint.

Analysis: Although the first phrase in the Vision may be a long view, the rest of the Vision would make a good Mission Statement, ". . . better, safer, and healthier life for people . . ." The Mission Statement of "Sustainable Growth" is more of a Goal but it does not appear to support the Vision. The second Mission refers to profit (value). The end of the statement "reducing our environmental footprint" could be a separate Mission.

University:

Vision: To be a leading university distinguished by its innovative spirit and premier baccalaureate college.

Mission: Educates students to lead and influence.

> **Analysis:** Is the Vision attainable? Is achieving distinction important to the customer or is it a marketing tool? Is the Mission more of a Function Statement to educate? Although the Mission alludes to educating students to lead and influence, I would prefer a stronger statement that its students will become leaders as a result of its educational programs. Students don't go to college for an education, they go to school to obtain the skills needed to achieve their vocation.

Community Nutrition Program:

Vision: To be a nutritionally aware community that fosters the development of healthy citizens.

Mission: Provide monetary and food assistance to schools and institutions participating in USDA Child Nutrition Programs enabling them to efficiently and attractively provide nutritious meals. The Division offers eligible participating organizations education, training, and technical assistance to ensure compliance with USDA regulations, policies, and instructions.

> **Analysis:** The Vision to make the community "aware" of good nutrition or to foster healthy citizens is a Mission that can be achieved.

The Mission describes Functions that could be Goals. These Functions will result in measurements of the monetary and food assistance to schools and not the better measurement of healthy citizens. This example shows the confusion created when trying to have both Vision and Mission Statements. If you get the Vision wrong, then the Mission will be wrong too.

Suggested Mission Statement: ***Improve the long-term health of our citizens through improved and attractive nutritional programs and meals.***

University:

Vision: To be the university of choice for natural and integrative health care. We promote conservative health care approaches that focus on the whole person. We provide leadership to develop collaborative and integrative health care models, support clinical research, prepare students for successful careers, and encourage lifelong learning in service to our community.

Mission: To advance and promote natural approaches to health through education, research, clinical services and community involvement.

> **Analysis:** The Vision and Mission are almost the same. It would make more sense if the titles were reversed. It appears the Vision describes how it will meet the Mission. I suggest combining both into a strong and concise Mission Statement. Also, we need to ask the "why" question. Why the need to advance and promote health? Improving the community's health should be the real Mission.
>
> Note that the last two elements in the Vision Statement, "prepare students for . . . and encourage . . . " are not contained

in the Mission Statement. As a result, there won't be any Goals supporting these important results. By creating just a Mission Statement, an organization can avoid these disconnects.

Circuit Court:

Vision: To be one truly independent and empowered branch of government providing a fair and responsive system of justice to lead the County into the twenty-first century.

Mission: To serve the public.

> **Analysis:** The Vision Statement implies that the court today is not independent, empowered, fair, or responsive because Vision describes a future status. The Mission Statement "To serve the public" is more of a motto or Function although it could be expanded to say something like, "Serve the public in a fair, impartial, and responsive manner" or "Continue to provide justice in a fair, impartial, and responsive manner." This may be a case of incorrectly injecting a core value into the planning statements.

Computer Company:

Vision: There will be a personal computer on every desk running our software.

Mission: Help people and businesses throughout the world realize their full potential.

> **Analysis:** The Vision could be a Mission, and the Mission could be a Vision. I think both are closer to being a Vision Statement. The Vision and Mission Statements could be combined into one Mission Statement, "Help people reach their full potential by making the best computers."

It appears that an attempt was made to create two different statements (Mission and Vision) in order to fulfill a requirement rather than a need to describe "attainable" and "not yet attainable" statements. It is obvious that only a Mission Statement is required.

Company:

Vision: To be the market leader and deliver the best value to our stakeholders.

Mission: To enhance profitability through innovative management strategies while ensuring cost effectiveness and harnessing creative ideas.

Analysis: The Vision concerns stakeholders while Mission focuses on profitability. Where is the customer in all this? A lot depends on the company's definition of "stakeholders." Who are the stakeholders? Customers, employees, suppliers, dealers, etc.? If "stakeholders" was replaced with "customers," then the Vision would make a good Mission Statement.

Business Consultant:

Vision: Every person has the support necessary to thrive as a small business owner.

Mission: Foster vibrant small business communities through mentoring and education.

Analysis: The Vision is more of a Mission Statement although vague. The Vision's key word is "thrive" but is it as a result of consulting? Can it be measured?. The Mission Statement sounds like a Function statement with the words "mentoring" and "education" which would represent Goals. What does the phrase "foster vibrant" really mean? And what does "communities" mean? Why not state the obvious Mission, "Help new and existing small businesses succeed."

Example of good a Vision and Mission Statement

Charity:

Vision: *Envisions* a world where all individuals and families achieve their human potential through education, income stability, and healthy lives.

Mission: *Improves lives* by mobilizing the caring power of communities around the world to advance the common good.

Goals:

- *Improve education and reduce* high school dropouts — 1.2 million students, every year — in half.
- *Help people achieve financial stability* and get 1.9 million working families — half the number of lower-income families who are financially unstable — on the road to economic independence.
- *Promote healthy lives* by increasing by one-third the number of youth and adults who are healthy and avoid risky behaviors.

Analysis: This is an excellent example of a proper set of Vision and Mission Statements. The Vision Statement is clearly a desired but not yet attainable end result. The Mission Statement is attainable and the Goals have the performance words, "improve lives," "help people," and "promote healthy lives" which can be measured for success. The Goals support the Mission to "improve lives" and not the Vision to "envision."

SUMMARY: The Vision Statement, because it is so broad and beyond the horizon, serves no purpose in real planning. Certainly, an agency's "vision" can be easily understood. The EPA wants an environment free of pollution, and the DOJ wants a crime-free society. The planning effort, however, cannot build a plan that accomplishes a Vision Statement. The EPA and DOJ must plan for actions that can be started and accomplished (e.g., reduce pollution and reduce crime). This same point of view applies to business and non-profit organizations. Their plans need to focus on what can be accomplished for the customer or client.

For fun, go back and list what you think should be the Goals and Objectives for all of the Mission Statement examples. When reading or viewing information about a company, non-profit organization, or government agency, ask yourself, "What should be the Mission?" This exercise will strengthen your ability to craft your own good Mission Statement and to evaluate an organization's ability to plan.

< >

APPENDIX C
GOVERNMENT PERFORMANCE AND RESULTS ACT (GPRA) OVERVIEW

In 1993, Congress enacted the GPRA (also known as the "Results Act") to establish a Strategic Planning and Performance Measurement process for the Federal Government's Executive Branch. Congress had grown tired of agencies receiving billions of dollars for long-term projects and then returning years later asking Congress for more money and time to finish the project. Congress decided it needed stricter accountability and tracking of agencies' project performance. If a project was failing, Congress wanted the opportunity to cancel it before wasting further funding on a failing project. The act was to improve effectiveness by focusing on the desired results that were legislated.

The Act also holds agencies more accountable. In recent years, the Office of Management and Budget (OMB) has required that the Senior Executive Service (SES) Personnel Appraisal Report include the SES Performance Appraisal Assessment Tool. This tool evaluates the SES employee's performance against the agency's Strategic Goals, as required by GPRA.

In working with this Act, I realized that it could easily be used by any organization. The planning methodology provides a sound basis for planning. The GPRA's Annual Performance Plan is the equivalent to a Tactical Plan. Its Annual Program Performance Plan Report provides a performance assessment for the organization. My approach differs from GPRA concerning the five-year requirement. As I've previously mentioned, restricting a plan to a time period prior to analysis is flawed.

The GPRA, however, does require agencies to visit their Strategic Plans at least once every three years. The creators of the GPRA knew that agencies would probably ignore their five-year plans unless they were required to visit the plan more frequently. It literally took and act of Congress to force agencies to pay closer attention to their Strategic Plans.

In the following description, I've edited, paraphrased, or removed parts of the GPRA to highlight only what is most important. To read the entire law, retrieve a copy from the Internet.

What is GPRA?

- A major culture change to focus on results, not intentions.

- Improvement in the management and budgeting framework:
    - Planning (with Congress and stakeholders)
    - Communicating
    - Decision-Making

- Hold management accountable for the following:
    - Money spent
    - Processes used
    - Outputs produced
    - Outcomes attained

GPRA's purpose:

- Improve the confidence of the American people (customer) in the capability of the Federal Government by holding Federal agencies accountable for achieving program results.

- Improve Federal program effectiveness and public accountability by promoting a new focus on results, service quality, and customer satisfaction.
- Help Federal managers improve service delivery by requiring that they plan for meeting program objectives and by providing them with information about program results and service quality.
- Improve congressional decision making by providing more objective information on achieving statutory objectives, and on the relative effectiveness and efficiency of Federal programs and spending.
- Improve internal management of the Federal Government.

The Strategic Plan should contain the following elements:

- Comprehensive Mission Statement.
- Description of general Goals and Objectives.
- How the general Goals and Objectives will be achieved.
- Relationship between Performance Goals in the annual Performance Plan and general Goals and Objectives in the Strategic Plan.
- Key factors (economic, demographic, social, or environmental) that could affect achievement of the general Goals and Objectives; certain conditions (events) not happening; and actions of Congress, other Federal agencies, and local governments.
- Description of program evaluations used and a schedule for future evaluations.

In developing a Strategic Plan:

- Look at the statutes and government policies and regulations.
- Involve managers at all levels.
- Assess internal and external environments.

- Identify core processes needed to implement Goals/Objectives/Strategies of the plan.

- Consult with Congress, customers, and other stakeholders potentially affected by or interested in the plan.

- Coordinate with other agencies with shared responsibilities, similar activities, or cross-agency programs.

Preparation and Submission of Strategic Plans: OMB Circular No. A-11 provides instructions for preparing Strategic Plans and highlights the relationship between Strategic Plans and Annual Performance Plans.

Annual Performance Plans - OMB Circular A-11, Part 6: GPRA requires each agency prepare an Annual Performance Plan covering each program activity as set forth in the agency budget.

- Performance Goals (Outputs and Outcomes): tangible, measurable targets and indicators for the fiscal year.

- Operational details. (resource needs and processes used)

- Clear Measures for comparing actual results with projected results.

- Means for verification and validation of measured results.

The annual Performance Plan shall:

- Establish Performance Goals to define the level of performance to be achieved by a program activity.

- Express such Goals in an objective, quantifiable, and measurable form.

- Briefly describe the operational processes, skills, and technology and the human, capital, information, or other resources required to meet the Performance Goals.

- Establish performance indicators to be used in measuring or assessing the relevant outputs, service levels, and outcomes of each program activity.

- Provide a basis for comparing actual program results with the established Performance Goals.

- Describe the means to be used to verify and validate measured values.

Annual Plans should strike a balance between too few and too many measures. Skimping on Performance Goals can produce a narrowly-drawn or fragmented picture of performance. Conversely, a plan loaded with measures blurs a reader's perspective over which Goals are essential for understanding program results. The set of Performance Goals included in an Annual Plan should be periodically modified as necessary to reflect changes in programs, agency ability to collect and report information, the importance and usefulness of any Goal, and other circumstances.

Annual Performance Reports - OMB Circular A-11, Part 6: GPRA requires each agency prepare an Annual Program Performance Report. The program performance report shall:

- Review the success of achieving the Performance Goals of the fiscal year.

- Evaluate the Performance Plan for the current fiscal year relative to the performance achieved toward the Performance Goals in the fiscal year covered by the report.

- Explain and describe where and why a Performance Goal has not been met; the plans and schedules for achieving the established Performance Goal; if the performance Goal is impractical or infeasible, why that is the case and what action is recommended.

- Describe actual performance achieved vs. Goals (targets) set for the year, including measurement data collected and analyzed.
- Explain any Goals that were not met.
- Describe a plan for achieving unmet Goals.
- Modify the current year's plan in light of previous year's performance.
- Describe performance information and trend data for at least the past four fiscal years.

Definitions

Strategic Goal or Strategic Objective: A statement of aim or purpose included in a Strategic Plan (required under GPRA). In a Performance Budget/Performance Plan, Strategic Goals should be used to group multiple program outcome Goals. Each program outcome Goal should relate to and in the aggregate be sufficient to influence the Strategic Goals or Objectives and their Performance Measures.

Program: A "program" shall be designated to include any organized set of activities directed toward a common purpose or Goal that an agency undertakes. The term may describe an agency's Mission, Functions, activities, services, projects, and processes and is defined as an organized set of activities directed toward a common purpose or Goal that an entity undertakes or proposes to carry out its responsibilities.

Performance Goal: A target level of performance over time expressed as a tangible, measurable Objective, against which actual achievement can be compared. A Performance Goal is comprised of a Performance Measure with targets and timeframes.

Performance Measures: Indicators, statistics, or metrics used to gauge program performance.

Target: Quantifiable or otherwise measurable characteristic that tells how well or at what level a program aspires to perform.

Output Measures: Outputs describe the level of activity that will be provided over a period of time, including a description of the characteristics (e.g., timeliness) established as standards for the activity. Outputs refer to the internal activities of a program (i.e., the products and services delivered). For example, an output could be the percentage of warnings that occur more than 20 minutes before a tornado forms.

Outcome Measures: Outcomes describe the intended result of carrying out a program or activity. They define an event or condition that is external to the program or activity and that is of direct importance to the intended beneficiaries and/or the public (the customer). For a tornado warning system, outcomes could be the number of lives saved and property damage averted. While Performance Measures must distinguish between outcomes and outputs, there must be a reasonable connection between them, with outputs supporting outcomes in a logical fashion.

Efficiency Measures: Effective programs not only accomplish their outcome Performance Goals, they strive to improve their efficiency by achieving or accomplishing more benefits for a given amount of resources. Efficiency measures reflect the economical and effective acquisition, utilization, and management of resources to achieve program outcomes or produce program outputs. They may also reflect ingenuity in the improved design, creation, and delivery of services to the public or customers by capturing the effect of intended changes made to outputs aimed to reduce costs and/or improve productivity, such as the improved targeting of products or services for simplified customer processing, manufacturability, or delivery.

Program Assessment: A determination, through Objective measurement and systematic analysis, of the manner and extent to which Federal programs achieve intended Objectives.

Performance Budget: A performance budget links strategic Goals with related long-term and annual Performance Goals (outcomes) as well as with the costs of specific activities to influence these outcomes about which budget decisions are made.

< >

APPENDIX D
VARIOUS OTHER PLANS AND ANALYSES

There are different approaches and techniques for conducting analyses. The techniques help to identify information and actions that will improve organizational performance. Not all of these approaches described below will be applicable to all organizations. Most of these techniques lean toward large, complex organizations that require in-depth evaluation of work processes and customer performance. Small organizations will find some techniques adequate for planning purposes without having to conduct significant effort. Remember, however, that good PRMs are usually difficult to obtain.

BUSINESS PLAN: Most businesses have a Business Plan. As a planning methodology, it lays out all the significant activities that need to be conducted when creating and managing a business. The plan contains subparts involving creating and managing the business, marketing and sales strategies, manufacturing efforts, administrative and financial aspects, hiring and managing employees, government regulations and paper work, etc. It is important to note that non-profit and government agencies can also use the Business Plan methodology.

I see Business Planning as an evolutionary process similar to Strategic Planning. A new and small organization's Business Plan has two parts:

- **Part One:** One-time events needed to start the organization, such as naming the organization, registering with the government, opening a bank account, buying insurance, etc.
- **Part Two:** The management, production, and delivery of the product and/or service.

Another version of the Business Plan may be needed for outside entities, such as when obtaining investors or bank loans. Generally, a Business Plan differs from a Strategic Plan by describing Functions and short-term actions that need to be accomplished. Whereas the Strategic Plan describes long-term actions. In fact, once the organization is up and running, the Business Plan may transition into a Tactical or Action Plan.

A good Business Plan guides a new organization to research, identify, analyze, and describe the actions needed for success. I have broken down the Business Plan into two parts: 1) Startup Plan and 2) Product Plan.

Overview: Describe your customer and the product (Mission Statement). How important is your product to the customer? Summarize your expertise to manage and deliver this product.

Startup Plan (actions to create the organization):
- Name the organization
- Designate the official mailing address
- Decide on the type of organization (e.g., sole proprietorship, non-profit, limited liability, small corporation)
- Register with IRS (Employer Identification Number), state, county, city governments where appropriate
- Select an accounting method (cash or accrual)
- Open a business bank account
- Obtain insurance
- Acquire the required physical space
- Obtain the office equipment
- Find funding for the organization
- Hire employees

- Identify all possible expenditures/expenses
- List the anticipated company growth
- Create company business forms
- List and contact the stakeholders

Product Plan (create and/or manage the product/service):

- Describe product(s) and/or service(s)
- Outline the effort required to create and deliver the product
- Assess the current and future targeted market
- Describe competing organizations and how successful they have been
- Determine how competing organizations promote products similar to yours
- Estimate the number and type of customers available for your product
- Evaluate the impact of social atmosphere, government regulations and fees, etc.
- Identify the product or organization's branding - where customers develop a positive emotional feeling and attachment towards the organization and its product
- Create a Marketing Plan to reach and keep customers
- Create a Sales Plan that describes the sales approach
- Identify all cost factors to determine wholesale and retail price of the product

The above list only provides a sample of topics. Each organization will have unique activities to address it's unique product or service.

STATISTICAL ANALYSIS: The term statistical analysis refers to methods used to look at information numerically. Among the many statistical methods are variance, boolean, cluster, multivariate, regression, scale, sequential, and others too numerous to list here. In regard to Strategic Planning, statistics should be as few and simple as possible. No one wants to wade through complex and multilayer tables and charts. The underlining work to obtain the key statistics should be placed in a separate document with a footnote in the plan. Don't burden your plan with worksheets. The reader only needs to know the results of the analysis. A footnote within the plan can direct the reader to the bulky, complicated, and wordy analysis document. This applies to all analyses.

TECHNOLOGY PLAN: Planning for future technology is difficult because technology continually changes. Industry leaders like Apple and Microsoft don't warn or prepare customers for the future technology solutions. Suddenly, there it is, Thunderbolt interface, retina screen, 3-D printing, solid state drive, etc. Your Strategic Plan created two years ago focused on standard PCs and servers to meet future requirements. Two years later, you have the Cloud, wireless access, small mobile devices, heavy Internet dependency, requirement for petabytes/exabytes of storage, new and different software applications and solutions, etc. It didn't occur over night but previous predictions soon became dated. Technology Plans need to be more flexible than Strategic Plans because technology changes rapidly. Sometimes you pick a technology solution knowing it's not the best answer but financially it made more sense. And some new technologies either flop (beta video and 8-track tapes) or become obsolete (floppy and CD disks, analog monitors).

Technology behaves differently than other commodities when it comes to price. Initially, new technologies start with a high price tag. Once the technology becomes mainstream, the price drops to a reasonable level while increasing performance. In 1991, a 100 megabyte hard drive cost $500 ($5 per megabyte). Today, a two or three terabyte hard drive costs under $100 ($.00005 per megabyte) and is many times faster and more reliable. Most common commodities don't change physically but their price fluctuates depending on supply and demand.

So, how do you identify your technology requirements for the future? Ask yourself, what will my customers need and what technology will help meet that need? What product will knock their socks off and can technology contribute to that desired result? In some cases technology can affect time, quality, cost, capability, efficiency, communication, accuracy, and probably a few other business elements.

Be careful, however, not to get so enamored with technology that you fail to bring real benefit to the customer. A friend once invested in a small company creating for third-world countries the ability to easily publish pamphlets containing instructions on using medicines and medical equipment in native languages. The company had a network of translators to convert English to native languages. Medical companies were interested in the concept. Unfortunately, the technology development consumed all of the company's investment funds before it could deliver the product. The company failed its Mission, and my friend lost his investment.

SWOT (Strengths, Weaknesses, Opportunities, and Threats): SWOT is a logical, common sense, and popular analysis tool. SWOT gathers internal and external information related to the organization. Usually mid- and large-sized organizations use SWOT analysis to determine how well they operate in the current work environment. Each section of the SWOT analysis contains specific information that helps managers evaluate the organization's overall performance. SWOT consists of four parts:

Strategic Planning Demystified

1. **Strengths:** The advantages that the organization has over its competition and the company's best-performing activities. Here are some examples:

   - Quality products
   - Good reputation with customers
   - Effective cost controls
   - Efficient production methods
   - Solid supply chains
   - Ability to adapt to new technologies
   - Sales force experienced in expanding sales to new markets
   - A lean but effective organizational structure
   - Experienced management staff
   - A near perfect Strategic Planning approach :)

   The organization's strengths are the elements, activities, talent, expertise, etc., that exceed other similar organizations. Here are samples of strengths that should be explored:

   - Competitive advantages
   - Resources, assets, people
   - Experience, knowledge, data, uniqueness
   - Financial reserves
   - Marketing reach, distribution, awareness
   - Innovative aspects
   - Geographical location
   - Price, value, quality
   - Accreditations, qualifications, certifications
   - Processes, systems, technology, communications

2. **Weaknesses:** Weakness is the opposite of Strength - what the organization is not doing or needs to improve. Weaknesses can include the following:

- High overhead costs
- Poor purchasing power
- Poor customer reputation
- Weak market and sales efforts
- Significant warranty returns
- Behind market trends
- Poor planning ability
- Bloated staffing levels

Once weaknesses are identified, an organization can eliminate or minimize their impact. Weaknesses can lose customers and income, so weaknesses need to be reduced if an organization is to be successful. The following are sample weaknesses that can be explored:

- Gaps in capabilities
- Lack of competitive strength
- Less-than-stellar reputation
- Poor financial condition
- Significant vulnerabilities
- Failing timelines and deadlines
- Lack of continuity with supply chain
- Poor morale, commitment, leadership
- Inefficient processes and systems
- Poor management of resources

3. **Opportunities:** A new set of conditions, actions, or elements that can become organizational strengths. Opportunities include the following:
   - Incorporate new technologies to product manufacturing
   - Use new marketing tools to increase consumers base
   - Access to low-interest business loan
   - Utilize local business courses to improve organization's management

   By identifying opportunities, the organization can apply or acquire the resources to exploit and implement these opportunities for success. Here are sample opportunities that can be explored:
   - Market developments
   - Competitors' vulnerabilities
   - Industry or social trends
   - Emerging technology
   - New tactics or business approaches
   - Business and product development
   - Innovation and research
   - Partnerships

4. **Threats:** The obstacles that the organization faces. Threat is the opposite of Opportunity. Threats can include the following:
   - Sudden negative changes in consumer demand or spending
   - Competitors with advanced features or lower prices
   - Spread of drug resistant viruses
   - New government regulations

Early threat detection can help avoid getting blindsided by negative changes. Once a threat has been identified, take action to avoid or overpower the threat. Threats look similar to Risks because they are the same. Here are sample threats that can be explored:

- Political and legislative effects
- Environmental effects
- Foreign competition
- Changing market
- New technologies
- Sustaining internal capabilities
- Retaining key staff
- Loss of financial backing
- Downturn in economy
- Seasonal and weather effects

The SWOT discloses positive and negative issues from which key actions can be formulated and proposed in support of organizational Goals and Objectives.

A word of caution. I have seen SWOT reports that identified significant issues that could help an organization. I have observed, however, organizations that simply inserted a SWOT list in their Strategic Plan with no analysis. Remember, the SWOT initiates analysis and formulates strategies to address issues, not just to create a list.

For example, items identified as weaknesses need to be analyzed and a decision made as to what action, if any, should be taken to avoid or offset the weakness. Simply stating the weakness is of no value until it is processed into some worthwhile corrective action. I found the following two weaknesses in a college Strategic Plan's long list of weaknesses:

- Verify that graduates are job ready
- No coffee machine

The first item disclosed a wonderful Performance Measurement that could validate and disclose the college's success to its students (customers). It would answer the question, is the college helping its students achieve their career or vocation (Mission)? Unfortunately, nowhere in the plan was there further discussion, analysis, Goal, or Performance Measure focusing on getting students ready for employment in their vocation.

The second item, no coffee machine, clearly proved that no one really understood SWOT nor took the time to analyze and list the most important issues for the college. The list contained every item managers submitted to the SWOT without selecting or vetting what was important. The school's management just wanted to check off a box (create a Strategic Plan) and get back to its Functions (teaching).

RISK ANALYSIS: This is a subpart found in many different plans and analyses. Although it might appear to be repetitive, I believe a separate discussion is needed to ensure that organizations understand its importance. I would define Risk Analysis as a decision process to take an action or make a decision with the potential of achieving equal or greater success for the organization but with the possibility of being the wrong action or decision.

There are several types of risks to be considered.

- An action in which the organization has full control. An action that changes an already accepted and relatively safe action, process, or condition. A short cut or different direction to achieve equal or greater success.

- Events where the organization has no initial control (e.g., competition, regulations, the marketplace, economy, weather).

A risk analysis relies on common sense. Humans conduct risk analysis every day. Should I drive home tonight in the snow or wait until tomorrow? Should I climb that cliff? Should I follow the doctor's orders to lose weight? Organizations take risks too. It is important to recognize the risk that goes along with a decision or action. Identifying the pros and cons to an action allows you avoid or reduce the risk.

SCENARIO PLANNING: Scenario Planning is day dreaming or sitting around the camp fire asking "what if" questions. What can be accomplished under what conditions? Can you expand business if you buy that manufacturing plant? Can you increase market share by networking with another organization? You want to make the right decision but there is no clear path to success. It is all vague with multiple choice decisions with the possibility that some decisions may be better or worse than others.

Under Scenario Planning, management lays out on paper the most plausible future scenarios. Each scenario is different from the other. Each scenario includes a risk against success. Analyzing the risks can help you decide if the risks are acceptable. Once a scenario is decided, it is critical to use an ongoing Strategic Planning process to turn the scenario into an achievable Goal or Objective.

PROTOTYPING: A process of duplicating a project on a small experimental scale to validate the development of a new process, system, procedure, etc. It reduces risk by first "dropping it to see if it breaks." Generally used in technology and manufacturing, it can be used in marketing against a select group of consumers to get their reaction.

Prototyping can either simply describe a process to test the waters or to build a model or mini-version. It initially takes time but can save significant resources later by not making mistakes on the larger, actual project. I participated in evaluating several multi-million dollar contracts using prototyping. It resulted in the successful implementation of new technologies.

BALANCED SCORECARD: Measures the financial, customer, business, and growth processes. It contains internal and external objective/subjective measurements. The Scorecard also measures operating income, capital financing processes, and the overall economic return for the organization. Customer measurements include customer satisfaction and retention. Business processes include production costs, product quality, and procurement methods. The Balance Scorecard reviews all aspects of a company for improvement. The Balanced Scorecard is complicated. I would only recommend this analysis for mid- and large-sized organizations.

BENCHMARKING, FORECAST, AND PREDICTIVE ANALYSIS METHODS: These three approaches are similar to each other. Each establishes a baseline to measure against future efforts to determine if an organization is being successful or not. For small organizations, benchmarking is essentially basic numbers from past performance, measured against current activities, to establish future estimates of performance. Forecast Analysis tracks current industry performance to identify future requirements. Predictive Analysis uses current and historic statistics to predict future trends and behaviors by the market, consumers, etc. These methods retrieve available data to determine future trends or behaviors. The various predictive models suggest where to find the data. Obvious trends become apparent, such as increase in warranty repairs, seasonal decrease in demand, etc. Whereas other trends may be difficult to identify or could be false.

VISION PLAN: Although not a part of the Strategic Plan, in some instances an organization might want to make a list of results that the organization would like to accomplish someday in the future. For example, an automobile manufacturer visualizing a day when cars will drive themselves without the interaction of humans. They would list the major elements required to accomplish this result, such as, roads and cars with sensors or GPSs that would allow safe travel to points selected by the passenger(s). Although an organization's Strategic Plan today would not include activities regarding a Vision, the Vision Plan could be part of any planning assessment to determine if the time had arrived to move the Vision into the Mission.

ONGOING MANAGEMENT TOOLS

The above analysis techniques help an organization to decide where it should be going. The following analysis tools help manage ongoing processes to identify the true cost and effort of such activities. These tools help to create the baseline from which future activities can be measured against. It can also be used to determine future costs of an activity so as to reduce cost overruns or uncertainties.

For small organizations, it may not be worth using all these tools. Understanding their concepts, however, may provide ideas on how to analyze the cost and effort in starting or operating a small organization.

ACTIVITY-BASED COSTING (ABC): ABC identifies and tracks all activities in terms of direct and indirect costs. ABC provides a more accurate and true cost analysis when determining the cost for current and future activities. It defines processes, identifies the cost drivers of those processes, determines a product's true unit cost, and creates reports that can be used to generate activity- or performance-based budgets.

Instead of using general cost numbers (government agencies tend to do this), ABC allows organizations to identify cause and effect relationships to objectively assign costs. ABC can disclose areas of high overhead costs per unit so that organizations can either reduce cost or increase the price for the product or service.

Some indirect costs may be difficult to identify but management can provide a best-guess figure. ABC provides an excellent analysis tool to identify and understand the true cost of doing business and ensure that the cost is passed onto the customer. In government and non-profit organizations, ABC helps to justify a budget and to build confidence that an agency can manage proposed new projects or responsibilities.

ABC avoids or minimizes cost distortions from arbitrary allocations of indirect costs. Unlike traditional line-item budgets which can't be tied to specific outputs, ABC generates useful information on how and where money is spent, cost effectiveness of each department, and provides a mechanism to benchmark for quality improvement.

Four Steps to ABC Implementation:

1. **Identify activities:** Perform an in-depth analysis of the operating processes of each component. Each process may consist of one or more activities required by outputs.

2. **Assign resource costs to activities:** Identify where costs occur. Here are three parts of costing:

    A. **Direct** - Costs that can be traced directly to one output.

    Example: Material and labor costs to build and assemble computers (motherboard, power supply, case, etc.).

    B. **Indirect** - Costs that benefit two or more outputs, but not all outputs.

Example: Costs for the tools/equipment used to build various types of computers, printers, etc.

C. **Overhead** - Costs that cannot be associated with any particular product. These costs may remain the same regardless of the products produced.

Example: Salaries for management and administrative personnel, building maintenance, plant security, employee benefit packages, etc.

3. **Identify outputs:** Identify the outputs for which an activity segment performs activities and consumes resources. Outputs can be products, services, or customers (persons or entities to whom an organization provides a product or service).

4. **Assign activity costs to outputs:** Activity drivers assign activity costs to outputs based on individual outputs' consumption or demand for activities. For example, a driver may be the number of times an activity is performed (transaction driver) or the length of time an activity is performed (duration driver).

ABC allows managers to identify the true costs to deliver a service or meet customer demand. It also improves operational efficiency and enhances decision-making through better, more meaningful cost information. Implementing ABC for large organizations will not be an easy task but once implemented, management will have solid information on the cost of conducting or increasing business. Whereas, small organizations can use the ABC concept to develop unit costs that include indirect or overhead costs.

I've seen ABC identify the true cost of a service which avoided over or under charging the customer. Traditionally, some organizations base service costs by the department in which a reimbursable activity existed. This approach, however, scooped up all organizational activities whether such costs related to the reimbursable activity or not. In addition, it missed the indirect or overhead costs expended by other sections in support of the activity. With ABC, you have a precise and accurate cost assessment related to reimbursable activities. A business understands this idea but non-profit and government agencies generally do not understand the value of ABC.

Another value to ABC is that it helps in identifying the true cost of proposed activities. With a good financial analysis, organizations can plan for future activities or expansion of existing current activities with greater confidence. ABC helps to avoid cost overruns because organizations can start off with good data on future costs. ABC supports Tactical Plans and in turn, supports the Strategic Plan.

EARNED VALUE: A method that tracks a specific project's performance, particularly for large technology contracts. An organization first analyzes and creates three estimates:

- **Effort:** The major activities needed to complete the project.
- **Time:** The time required for each major activity to complete the project.
- **Cost:** The cost for each major activity.

The total estimates for effort, time, and cost should cover all project activities. The project activities usually are in chronological order although there can be exceptions. Each activity is assigned an estimated effort, time, and cost. Once the project begins, the project manager reports on the progress for these three estimates as the project continues. The progress report is usually reported on a weekly or monthly basis. Actual progress is measured against planned progress.

- **Effort:** The amount of work (activity) exerted to date.
- **Time:** The amount of scheduled time that has been expended.
- **Cost:** The amount of money that has been spent.

This approach is particularly useful when creating Objectives and Strategies in support of a Goal. A component will make a reasonable and educated guess as to the amount of effort, time, and cost to achieve an Objective or Strategy. Once a component begins work on the Objective or Strategy, Earned Value ensures that the effort stays on track. If cost begins to rise or schedule begins to slip, actions can be taken to correct the problem or at least reassess the original assumption to make a decision to continue, change, or to cease the project.

As mentioned earlier in this book, I used Earned Value in assessing contract activities. It occurred to me that Earned Value could easily be adapted to managing large internal projects and activities within an organization. The contractors working for the government are required to plot out the effort, time, and cost of a project to ensure that the project is completed as required. Why not use the same methodology within a business, non-profit, or government organization?

CONFIGURATION MANAGEMENT (CM): CM ensures that changes made to business activities, technology, manufacturing, marketing, or other organization activities won't cause an unplanned negative impact to another part of the organization. An example would be an effort to increase sales using a new marketing strategy. The production manager would need to be consulted to ensure that if the new sales strategy works, the organization's production capacity can meet the increased sales.

ROLLING ANALYSIS: A rolling analysis collects data over a moving period of time and averages its performance. The analysis adds a new data point as it arrives, and discards the oldest data point. For example, you take the sales for the most recent 90-day period. The next day you add the sales for the new day and drop the sales for the oldest day in the measured period of time. You then divide the total 90 day sales number by 90 to provide the daily average. You then chart the average to compare against previous daily averages. In time, this gives you a stable trend analysis. The longer the measured time period, the more stable the trend.

An advantage of a rolling analysis is that short-term anomalies have less influence on the overall averaging. For example, comparing months is unequal because some months have 29, 30, and 31 days. Some months have several holidays while other months have none. Some months have snow days while others do not. These inequities can cause false assumptions. The rolling analysis also disregards fiscal or calendar events that unfairly influence trend analysis.

The period of time to be measured is determined by the volume and ease in obtaining the data. An organization may want to measure by months or years (which requires a longer period of time to reveal trends). The rolling analysis provides an early indication of success or failure whereas traditional long-term, fixed timed measurements do not provide information until the end of the measured period of time to determine an organization's status.

A rolling statistic provides a stable and meaningful indicator for current and future performance. Traditional statistical tracking, such as the FBI's Uniform Crime Report (UCR), is corralled by the calendar year and only provides a view of dated, past performance. Yes, over several years, certain crime statistics indicate either a rise or fall of certain crimes.

Strategic Planning Demystified

Unfortunately, you need to wait a year before you know where the trend is going. If a crime statistic begins to increase in November and December, it may take over a year before its growth is reflected in the UCR. Whereas, a rolling statistic would give you a much earlier indication of change. This early warning of a changing, long-term trend will help to address a growth in a particular crime activity. For any organization, a rolling analysis provides an opportunity to surface negative trends early enough to do something about it.

CONTINUITY PLAN (preparing for disasters): An organization's lack of preparedness for future negative incidences can jeopardize the organization's core Mission and its long-term health. A Continuity Plan identifies and documents potential internal and external threats to the organization. The plan provides details on how to protect or reduce the impact if a negative incident occurs. The plan helps the organization counter a threat before it takes down the organization. The effectiveness of the Continuity Plan rests with the ability of an organization to identify threats. What happens if you have an interruption of electricity, delivery of services or supplies, or access to the Internet?

Today's technology poses some of the greatest threats. Do you have a reliable backup data system. How fast can you replace failed servers? How can you protect your data from hackers? I have talked to numerous small businesses that use computers for bookkeeping, billing, etc. I am always surprised to learn that many times there is no backup system. If a tornado destroys your office building, how fast can you recover? You need to have answers before and not after the negative event.

For some businesses, having a complete Disaster Recovery Plan may not be an achievable option because of the cost or the nature of the business. A small store's ability to recover from a disaster can be very limiting. A sole proprietorship business ceases to exist if the owner dies or becomes ill. For larger organizations, however, creating a Continuity Plan should be feasible and should be seriously considered.

CUSTOMER SURVEY: For an organization to meet customer requirements or needs, an organization needs to know its customer. Marketing surveys are common among businesses. Non-Profit and government agencies usually have advisory boards or councils to provide guidance. Existing organizations can establish methods to survey customers' satisfaction. New organizations have the difficult task of identifying and locating potential customers. The following list contains suggested topics to explore.

- Describe your customer
- Conduct market survey to determine the type, number, and availability of customers
- Identify the ways to contact customers
- Conduct electronic statistical profiles of customers where possible
- Determine if the customer is satisfied with your competition's performance
- Determine where the customer wants or needs to go
- Determine where you can take the customer in the future

SUMMARY: A good analysis helps to formulate a good Mission Statement and the supporting Goals, Objectives, and Strategies. The analysis tools described above can help organizations determine how they are performing internally and externally, and where they need to go in relationship to the customer. It is important to note that almost all of the above tools and examples help to identify risk factors.

www.ingramcontent.com/pod-product-compliance
Lightning Source LLC
Chambersburg PA
CBHW071413170526
45165CB00001B/262